66
Ways
to
Better
Days

66
Ways
to Better
Days

Practices in Law and Life
for Busy Professionals

Pamela Michelle, J.D., M.S.

66 Ways to Better Days:
Practices in Law and Life for Busy Professionals

Copyright © 2017
Pamela Michelle

Publisher
Come Into Your OWN Publishing, a subsidiary of
Business Over Coffee International (BOCI)
5865 Ridgeway Center Pkwy Ste 300
Memphis, Tennessee 38120
www.comeintoyourown.com
info@comeintoyourown.com

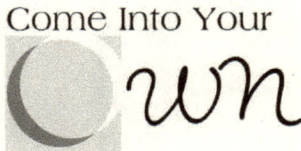

Come Into Your
Own

Cover photography by Andrea Blakesberg Photography
Cover design by Sherri D. Motes
Edited by Bethany Sledge

First edition: August 2017

Contents

Preface

First, a note about the image you will see throughout this book. It depicts what is known as a Mudra, a gesture often utilized in yoga and/or meditation practice. Practicing these various hand postures is known to be a useful way to affect the body's meridians/fields of energy and to turn attention inward to the body, thus fine-tuning your body awareness. Furthermore, many Mudras have beautiful meaning, and to focus on the meaning is very thought-provoking. I find the symbolism or meaning of a Mudra to be a poignant and literal depiction of how one can take his or her well-being into his or her own hands. That is what this book is all about.

In both law and life, there is a constant challenge to attempt to control external circumstances without allowing this to result in constant mood fluctuations and even our perception of ourselves. For this purpose, mindfulness is introduced in several of the sections of this book as a practice that teaches us to be fully present, aware of where we are and what we are doing, and not overly reactive or overwhelmed at what is going on around us. When our mind takes "flight" we lose touch with our body, and pretty soon we are engrossed in obsessive thoughts about something that just happened or concern about the future. Mindfulness recognizes and cultivates the best of who we are as human beings—it's all about paying attention in the present moment. Left to itself, the mind wanders through all kinds of thoughts, including those expressing anger or craving depression, revenge, or self-pity. As we indulge in these kinds of thoughts, we reinforce those emotions in our hearts and cause ourselves to suffer. Mostly, these thoughts are about the past or future. Since the past no longer exists and the future is just a fantasy until it happens, the current moment is the one that should never be avoided.

To further emphasize, your brain and body are remarkable things. While emotion is something that we rely on from moment to moment, the reality is that the physiological mechanism behind emotion lasts only ninety seconds. If it lasts longer than this, it is because we have chosen to rekindle it. If the emotion is a challenging one, body, speech, and mind become engaged in running away from the feeling, which essentially keeps it going and going. The point here is again to help you to recognize the power of your own mind and how you can leverage some of the techniques offered within this book to improve each moment of your life and have better days as a result.

There are sixty-six sections in this book to emphasize how long it takes for us to form a new behavior that then becomes automatic. If a habit does not include addictive additives or stimulants, which make the withdrawal and brain processes different, you can take the habit out of your life the same way you put one into your life. In this manner, you will find yourself free of the unconscious—and many times detrimental—patterns that have their costs.

My hope for each reader of this book is that you will find new ways to create more equanimity in your days by trying any of the suggestions outlined in these sixty-six sections. This book is designed to be consciously utilized. While information can be powerful, without implementation it can be quickly forgotten and even considered a poor use of effort or time. There are places for you to take notes within this book, which I encourage you to utilize and to indicate the sections that you find most intriguing or useful in your daily life. My hope is that you will keep this book on your desk and work with it daily or as often as time permits.

With profound gratitude I invite you into deeper relationship with yourself.

Blessings on your journey,

Pamela Michelle

1

The Transformative Power of Music

"Music washes away from the soul
the dust of everyday life."
~Berthold Auerbach

Music can deliver much-needed relief during the work-day, in times of high stress, for periods when you want to be more creative in your work, or simply at a moment of connection to your best self.

How to use music during your workday:

- Make your playlist from songs you already know, and if your tasks involve linguistic processing, focus on lyric-free options.
- If you have something to learn or you need motivation for a project, pump up your mood with music *before* you get started.
- If you are working on a repetitive task, music will help you perform faster and make fewer errors.
- Music affects how you interact with your coworkers in that if you feel better, you usually are more respectful, patient, and cooperative.
- Listening to music that is unfamiliar to you may ultimately compromise your work focus.
- When you're trying to learn something at work, it is best to turn off your music, particularly if you are

learning verbally or through reading and the music has lyrics.

For those who appreciate knowing why, consider this:

- Music triggers the release of feel-good neurotransmitters, which help you to feel relaxed and happy and therefore to focus better.
- Music can also be helpful if you must work in a noisy workspace. Noisy environments increase levels of stress hormones and decrease levels of feel-good neurotransmitters such as dopamine. Those changes negatively affect the prefrontal cortex, hindering executive function.
- Data processing takes energy you could use to focus on your job, so music can help block out the excessive input that could overwhelm you.

Reflections

_____

_____

_____

_____

_____

_____

_____

_____

_____

_____

_____

_____

2

Decision~making Habits

"The thing that will make you most tired
is the decision you haven't made."
~Pam Olsen

However we feel about them, decisions form a large part
of our workday.

- Making decisions helps you to overcome activating
  certain parts of the brain that may pull you toward
  negative impulses and routines.
- Making decisions changes your perception of the
  world; finding solutions to your problems calms your
  nervous system.
- Brain science shows that making decisions reduces
  worry and anxiety, as well as helping to resolve
  problems.

But wait! Deciding can be hard, especially in the legal
profession. So what kind of decisions should you make?
Neuroscience has an answer!

- Make a "good enough" decision. Being a perfectionist
  can be stressful, and brain studies back this up. Let's
  face it; there are rarely perfect decisions in the "practice" of law.

- Trying to be perfect overwhelms your brain with emotions and will ultimately make you feel out of control.
- Deciding also boosts pleasure! (Actively choosing causes changes in attention circuits in the brain and increases the decision maker's positive feelings about the activity.)
- So make more decisions! Neuroscience researcher Alex Korb sums it up nicely: " We don't just choose the things we like; we also like the things we choose."

Reflections

_____

_____

_____

_____

_____

_____

_____

_____

_____

_____

_____

3

How to Express Negative Emotions

"Unexpressed emotions never die. They are buried alive and will come forth later in uglier ways."
~Sigmund Freud

Don't suppress your negative emotional experiences.

- "You feel awful? Okay, give that awfulness a name!" Sad? Anxious? Angry? Scientists have found that people who try to suppress a negative emotional experience fail to do so.
- While people suppressing emotions thought they looked fine, the part of their brain that controls basic emotions was just as aroused as without suppression and in some cases more aroused.
- Trying not to feel something doesn't work and in some cases even backfires.

Labeling is a fundamental tool of mindfulness. You merely need to use a few words to describe an emotion and ideally use symbolic language such as indirect metaphor.
Here's the bottom line:

- Describe the emotion in just a word or two, and it helps to reduce the emotion.

Reflections

_____

_____

_____

_____

_____

_____

_____

_____

_____

_____

_____

4

The Power in Your Breath

"When you own your breath,
nobody can steal your peace."
~Author unknown

During stressful situations, we begin to breathe rapidly and shallowly from our upper lungs. This can cause dizziness, shortness of breath, confusion, and even nausea. The good news is that by changing your breathing you can reverse these symptoms and stimulate the body's relaxation (parasympathetic) response.

Benefits of proper breathing:

- Blood pressure decreases.
- Muscle tension decreases.
- One has a growing sense of ease in the body and calmness in the mind.

Calming Breath
(at least thirty seconds)

- Take a long, slow breath in through your nose, first filling your lower lungs, then your upper lungs.
- Hold your breath to the count of three.
- Exhale slowly through pursed lips, while you relax the muscles in your face, jaw, shoulders, and stomach.

Practice this calming breath at least ten times a day for several weeks. Use it between projects, when you want to release tension, or if you need a sense of calmness.

Calming Counts
(at least ninety seconds)

- Take a long, deep breath and exhale it slowly while saying the word "relax" silently.
- Close your eyes.
- Let yourself take ten natural, easy breaths. Count down with each exhale, starting with ten.
- When you reach one, open your eyes.

For the maximum benefit, concentrate on the breathing and not on your worried thoughts.

Reflections

_____

_____

_____

_____

_____

_____

_____

_____

_____

_____

_____

5

From a Negative Feeling: What's Next?

> "You cannot have a positive life
> in a negative mind."
> ~Joyce Meyer

In our previous tips, we suggested that you label your emotions as they arise, especially when they are challenging, so as not to suppress them. However, this is far different than complaining, which is bad for your brain and your health.

Here are a few ways that complaining harms your health:

- When your brain is firing off synapses of anger, for example, you are weakening your immune system.
- You are raising your blood pressure.
- In addition, you increase your risk of heart disease, obesity, and diabetes due to higher levels of the stress hormone cortisol.

Having a negative thought makes it easier for you to have that thought again. It gets worse, too. Not only do repetitive negative thoughts make it easier to think more negative thoughts, they also make it more likely that negative thoughts will occur to you just walking down the street. Not only does hanging out with your own negative thoughts rewire your brain for negativity, but hanging out with negative people does much the same.

- Through repetition of thought, you've brought the pair of synapses that represent your negative proclivities closer together, and when the moment arises for you to form a thought . . . the thought that wins is the one that has the less distance to travel. Thus, gloom soon outpaces positivity.
- So why does hanging out with negative people rewire your brain for negativity? When we see someone experiencing an emotion, our brain "tries out" that same emotion to imagine what the other person is going through. The brain does this by attempting to fire the same synapses in your brain so that you can attempt to relate to the emotion you are observing. In the positive sense, this is basically empathy. It is also how we get to mob mentality. By example, it is our shared bliss at a great music concert, but it can also be your night at happy hour with your friends who love to complain constantly. Surround yourself with happy people who rewire your brain toward positivity.

Reflections

_____

_____

_____

_____

_____

_____

_____

_____

_____

_____

_____

6

Calming Anxiety

"Anxiety is a thin stream of fear trickling through
the mind. If encouraged, it cuts a channel
into which all other thoughts are drained."
~Arthur Somers Roche

Many strategies are available to help a person overcome anxiety. The strategies listed below fall into three categories: behavioral, cognitive, and physical. You may find that some strategies work in some circumstances but not in others, and what helps you may not benefit someone else. Experiment to observe what works best and when.

- Clean your desk or your workspace. Physical order often helps us fill a sense of mental order.
- Do a project you have been putting off, such as a phone call or an email.
- If someone else's behavior has triggered anxiety for you, try accepting that you may never know the full reason or background behind the person's behavior.
- Look back on the anxiety-provoking situation you are in from a point in the future; e.g., six months from now. Does the problem seem smaller when you view it from further away?
- If you are imagining a negative outcome to something you are considering, also imagine a positive outcome.

- Jot down three things you worried about in the past that didn't come to pass.
- If you rarely back out of commitments and feel overwhelmed by your to-do list, try giving yourself the permission to say you can no longer do something you previously agreed to do.
- Scratch something off your to-do list for the day either by getting it done *or* by clearly deciding not to do that task today.
- Forgive yourself for not handling a situation in an ideal way, including interpersonal situations. Then ask yourself what's the best thing you can do to move forward in a positive way.
- Question your social comparisons. Accept that there is a gap between your real self and your ideal self and also that comparing yourself only to the most successful person you know may not be a fair representation.

Reflections

_____

_____

_____

_____

_____

_____

_____

_____

_____

_____

_____

7

The Restorative Power of Sleep

"Silence is the sleep that nourishes wisdom."
~ Francis Bacon

Sleep is a complex biological process that depends heavily on our environment and behavior, which is a good thing because we can impact it. Unfortunately, our twenty-first-century American lifestyles and homes make it very easy to counteract the biological process of falling asleep. So here are tips for a perfect bedtime routine, based on neuroscience.

- Create a recognizable pattern/bedtime routine so your brain recognizes the time for sleep.
- Dim the lights and black out your bedroom. Avoid all lit screens for an hour before you want to fall asleep.
- Put your mind at ease by preparing for tomorrow; for example, by packing a bag for work and writing a to-do list.
- Keep your sleeping quarters cool; an average of 65 to 68 degrees is most effective. (We actually can't fall asleep until our body temperature drops sufficiently.)
- Meditate your way to sleep.

Sit at the end of your bed with good but relaxed posture, with eyes closed. Take deep, full breaths, simply noticing the sensations going in and out

Count *after* each breath. Make your way up to ten and then back down to one.

- Be consistent with your timing, starting your routine at a similar time every day.
- Make your routine enjoyable. Like all things, if you are enjoying the process, you are more likely to meet your goals.

Reflections

_____

_____

_____

_____

_____

_____

_____

_____

_____

_____

_____

8

Four Ways to Clear Your Mind

"Clear your mind of thoughts
that no longer serve you."
~Author unknown

Succeeding in almost any area of life, including competitive sports, relies on mastering your mind-set. One of the most important skills to learn in controlling one's mental state is to clear the mind of unwanted thoughts.

- Distraction: Neuroscientists have confirmed that the key to "optimal inattention" lies in occupying your mind with something else through distraction. The mind can only think of one thing at a time.
- Suppression: It turns out that modern brain imaging technology has identified the ways in which the brain forgets unwanted memories. Knowing that the brain has the distinct ability to forget may be helpful and explains how individuals can cope with negative or traumatic events.
- Substitution: Although the strategies of suppression and substitution are found to be equally effective, substitution is the process of voluntarily forgetting unwanted memories.
- Meditation: Neurologists are beginning to recognize that meditation will change people's brains. In one

researcher's anxiety study, the subjects reported decreases in everyday anxiety by as much as 39 percent after practicing meditation.

Reflections

_____

_____

_____

_____

_____

_____

_____

_____

_____

_____

9

Better Days in Your Law Practice

> "Gratitude can transform common days
> into thanksgivings, turn routine jobs
> into joy, and change ordinary
> opportunities into blessings."
> ~William Arthur Ward

Intentionally notice the pleasantness around you.

- Neuroscience-based stress relief: Take in the good!
- Have you ever noticed how much more weight the negative things that happen to us carry than the positive ones do?

"Your brain preferentially scans for, registers, stores, recalls, and reacts to unpleasant experiences; it's like Velcro for negative experiences and Teflon for positive ones" (Rick Hanson, neuropsychologist).

- So in a nutshell, this means that noticing the good, focusing on it, and turning up the volume on your experience of it are the best things you can do.

Reflections

_____

_____

_____

_____

_____

_____

_____

_____

_____

_____

_____

10

Become Mindful

Mindfulness is:

- Noticing your thoughts, feelings, and actions without judgment or criticism.
- Observing what's happening around you.
- Being fully aware of your senses moment to moment.
- Living in the here and now without resorting to old patterns and automatic reactions.
- Exercising acceptance of your own experience, whether good, bad, or neutral.
          (Jonathan S. Kaplan, PhD)

Here are mindfulness activities you can practice:

- Sometimes we can find the best mindfulness coaches right in our own homes. Pets and children have an uncanny ability to live fully in the present moment; thus, they can serve as miniature mindfulness masters to guide our practice.

Exercising Acceptance

- "It just is what it is" can be a useful mantra.
- We should free ourselves of comparisons to others or to our past selves.

- Be grateful for as much as possible, such as health or the ability to move your body.
- Accept your limits.
- Get out in nature. Being surrounded by nature is very good for us. Research has demonstrated that walking in a park boosts our mood and even our ability to concentrate.

Create a mindfulness first-aid kit.

- For a visual, pick a pleasant picture.
- For taste, pick something with a long shelf life like chocolate.
- For sound, consider calming songs or prayer.
- For touch, select an object with a notable texture, like a piece of fabric or a rock.
- For smell, select anything from essential oils to something you find pleasant like coffee beans.

Reflections

_____

_____

_____

_____

_____

_____

_____

_____

_____

_____

_____

_____

11

Embracing Free Time

"Nothing is a waste of time unless you think it is."
~Marty Rubin

The truth is, work expands to fill the time it's given, and for most of us, we could spend considerably fewer hours at the office and still get the same amount done.

The problem comes when we spend so much of our time frantically chasing productivity that we refuse to take real breaks. We put off sleeping in, going for a long walk, or reading a book for pleasure. Even if we do manage time away from our "responsibilities," it often comes with the thought about what we should be doing, so the experience is ruined by a feeling of guilt. Instead, there may be a habit of turning to the least fulfilling activity of them all: sitting at our desk, browsing websites, and contributing to neither our happiness nor our productivity.

The why:

"There is an idea we must always be available, work all the time," according to Michael Guttridge, a psychologist who focuses on workplace behavior. "It's hard to break out of that and decide to go to the park." The downsides are obvious according to Guttridge: we end up zoning out at the computer, looking for distraction on social media, and telling ourselves we are "multi-tasking" while really spending far longer than necessary on the most basic tasks. In this regard, we are missing out on the mental and physical benefits of time focused on ourselves. "Wasting time is about recharging your battery and decluttering," he explained. Taking time to be totally, gloriously, proudly unproductive will ultimately make you better at your job, says Guttridge, but it is also fulfilling in and of itself.

Reflections

_____

_____

_____

_____

_____

_____

_____

_____

_____

_____

_____

_____

12

A Primer on Color

> "All colors are the friends of their neighbors
> and the lovers of their opposites."
> ~Marc Chagall

Colors relate respectively to the body, the mind, the emotions and the essential balance between these three. The psychological properties of some of the colors with the most positive effects are as follows:

BLUE: Intellectual

Positive aspects: Intelligence, communication, trust, efficiency, serenity, duty, logic, coolness, reflection, calm.

The color of the mind, blue is essentially soothing; it affects us mentally rather than physically. Strong blues will stimulate clear thought, and lighter, soft blues calm the mind and aid concentration. It is the color of clear communication.

YELLOW: Emotional

Positive aspects: Optimism, confidence, self-esteem, emotional strength, friendliness, and creativity.

Yellow is the strongest color psychologically. Soft yellows will lift our spirits and our self-esteem; it is the color of confidence and optimism.

GREEN: Balance

Positive aspects: Harmony, balance, rest, restoration, reassurance, peace.

Being in the center of the color spectrum, green is the color of balance, and thus it is reassuring on the most primitive level.

VIOLET: Spiritual

Positive aspects: Spiritual awareness, vision, luxury, authenticity, and truth.

This color is often described as purple. It takes awareness to our higher level of thought, even, some would say, into the realm of spiritual values. It encourages deep contemplation or meditation and usually communicates the finest possible quality.

BLACK

Positive aspects: sophistication, security, emotional safety, efficiency.

Many psychological implications lie in the fact that black is all colors, totally absorbed. It creates protective barriers as it helps absorb all the energy coming toward you. It transmits absolute clarity, with no fine nuances. It engenders sophistication and works particularly well with white.

Reflections

_____

_____

_____

_____

_____

_____

_____

_____

_____

_____

_____

13

Utilizing Walking Meditation

"One of the most useful and grounding ways
of attending to our body is the practice
of walking meditation."
~Jack Kornfield

Walking meditation is a simple and universal practice for developing calm, connectedness, and embodied awareness. The benefit of walking meditation is to use the natural movement of walking to cultivate clearer presence.

How to begin a walking meditation practice:

- Select a quiet place where you can walk comfortably back and forth, indoors or out, about ten to thirty paces in length.
- Open your senses to see and to feel your whole surroundings with your feet firmly planted on the ground. Center yourself, and feel how your body is standing on the earth.
- Begin to walk a bit more slowly than usual. Pay attention to your body, and with each step feel the sensations of lifting your foot and leg off the earth. Then, mindfully place your foot back down. Feel each step as you walk.
- Continue to walk back and forth for ten or twenty minutes or more. Your attention may wander many

times, and as soon as you notice this, just acknowledge it softly in your mind and return to the next step.

Use the walking meditation to calm and to collect yourself and to live more wakefully in your body. You can practice your mindful walking anywhere and learn to enjoy walking for its own sake.

Reflections

_____

_____

_____

_____

_____

_____

_____

_____

_____

_____

14

Incorporating Exercise

"Take care of your body.
It's the only place you have to live."
~Jim Rohn

For most healthy adults, the Department of Health and Human Services recommends these exercise guidelines:

- Aerobic activity. Get at least 150 minutes of moderate aerobic activity or 75 minutes of vigorous aerobic activity a week, or some combination of the two. The guidelines suggest that you spread out this exercise through the week.
- Strength training. Do strength training exercises for all major muscle groups at least two times a week. Aim to do a single set of each exercise, using a weight or resistance level heavy enough to tire your muscles after about twelve to fifteen repetitions.

Reducing sitting time is important, too. The more hours you sit each day, the higher your risk of metabolic problems, even if you achieve the recommended amount of daily activity.

Short on long chunks of time? Even brief bouts of activity offer benefits. For example, if you can't fit in one thirty-minute walk, try three ten-minute walks instead.

Reflections

_____

_____

_____

_____

_____

_____

_____

_____

_____

_____

_____

15

Plants in Your Workspace

> "What is a weed? A plant whose
> virtues have never been discovered."
> ~Ralph Waldo Emerson

There are proven health benefits, both physiological and psychological, to having living plants in your home or office environment.

- Increased happiness. Research has shown that the presence of plants leads to a reduction of stress and increases feelings of well-being with a marked improvement in mood and self-esteem.
- Lower blood pressure. Studies performed in a hospital setting indicate that those with plants in their rooms had lower blood pressure and heart rates.
- Air purification. Plants have the ability to purify the air and even extend to removing the pollutants contained in cigarette smoke. A peace lily in particular is an excellent choice.
- Humidifying the air. Plants are natural humidifiers in that breathing moisture is helpful for preventing dryness in the skin, throat, nose, and lips and can help ward off cold and flu symptoms.
- Improved mental health. Caring for something living is great therapy when feeling depressed or lonely. Pets

aren't allowed in many places, but plants are a great alternative.

- Sharper focus and mental acuity. By increasing the oxygen in the air you breathe and removing pollutants, plants improve your concentration and memory, heighten awareness, and increase creativity.

With a minimal initial outlay and no ongoing costs, living with plants could well be the best decision you've ever made for your health.

Reflections

_____

_____

_____

_____

_____

_____

_____

_____

_____

_____

_____

16

Incorporating a Gratitude Practice

"Gratitude turns what we have into enough."
~Author unknown

When we are feeling stuck, it's hard to see the positive forces; we are more focused on obstacles and perhaps even fears. This is exactly when gratitude is warranted. Gratitude helps us see our situation in a new way and opens us to new solutions. The reality is, we aren't naturally hard-wired to be grateful, so for most people, it actually requires practice.

According to Dr Robert Emmons, there are three stages to cultivating the gratitude practice:

1. Recognizing what we are grateful for.
2. Acknowledging it.
3. Appreciating it.

The benefits of practicing gratitude can be truly life altering, and here are some helpful tips and examples:

- Keep a gratitude journal. All this requires is noting on a daily basis one or more things for which you are grateful.
- Vow not to complain, criticize, or gossip for a week. This will help you realize how much energy you are spending on negative thoughts.

- When you find yourself in a challenging situation, ask: What can I learn? When I look back on this without emotion, what will I be grateful for?
- At least one time a day share your appreciation of something or someone.

Reflections

_____

_____

_____

_____

_____

_____

_____

_____

_____

_____

_____

_____

17

Recognizing and Perceiving Burnout

"Burnout is nature's way of telling you,
you've been going through the motions,
your soul has departed."
~Sam Keen, *Fire in the Belly*

Burnout can be defined as the exhaustion of physical or emotional strength or motivation, usually as a result of prolonged stress or frustration.

Paul Davis-Laack, J.D., has identified seven strategies to prevent burnout.

1. Increasing your self-efficacy. Self-efficacy is having the belief in your own ability to accomplish meaningful goals and tasks personally. The most direct and effective way to enhance self-efficacy is by mastering experiences through performance, setting goals that are achievable, and then being mindful of your ability to achieve what you set out to do. These create an environment for you to ask yourself, "What else can I do?"
2. Identify what you need from your work. If you can identify the virtues of an ideal situation, you can more likely cultivate these experiences.
3. Have creative outlets. Even if your work does not afford you opportunities to express yourself creatively,

having some type of creative outlet will help keep you engaged and motivated.

4. Take care of yourself. Work can feel like there is always something to do, but the reality is whatever "it" is will still be there after you have taken a much-needed break.

5. Get support where you can find it. Though it takes time and effort to maintain social connections, having supportive people in our lives is the best inoculation against burnout.

6. Get real and go there! There is necessary and possibly tough internal and external soul-searching when burnout occurs. Really digging into the why of what you are doing and what isn't working is key to reconnecting with your core values.

7. Increase your positive emotions. Positive emotions build resilience, creativity, and the ability to be solution focused. Aim for a ratio of positive emotions to negative emotions of at least three to one, which is the point where a person will start experiencing increased resilience and happiness.

Reflections

_____

_____

_____

_____

_____

_____

_____

_____

_____

_____

_____

18

The Benefits of Volunteering

> "We can't help everyone,
> but everyone can help someone."
> ~Ronald Reagan

Perhaps the most tangible benefit of volunteering is the satisfaction of incorporating service into your life and making a difference in the life of another. When we share our time and talents, we:

- Solve problems.
- Strengthen communities.
- Improve lives.
- Connect to others.
- Transform our own lives.

Volunteering also has health benefits. There is a strong relationship between volunteering and health, which includes lower mortality rates, greater function ability, and lower rates of depression. It is noted that volunteers who devote at least one hundred hours a year to volunteer activities are those most likely to exhibit these positive outcomes.

Reflections

_____

_____

_____

_____

_____

_____

_____

_____

_____

_____

_____

19

The Value of Learning New Things

"Self-education is lifelong curiosity."
~Lailah Gifty Akita

Learning has benefits that extend far beyond simply obtaining knowledge.

- Learning more things makes you more confident. Learning new things keeps your mind sharp, and by doing that you will be able to navigate through life with much more ease.
- Your brain is like a muscle, and as with every other muscle, the principle applies: "Use it, or lose it!"
- If you are doing things out of habit only, you decrease the likelihood of expanding your brain's capacity. Learning new things, even if it feels challenging at first, helps the brain perform in peak condition.
- Stop to think about what things you want to learn and start now. Start small, even fifteen minutes every day for thirty days, and you will see improvement in yourself and keep going.
- Our brain is a great machine, and it actually tries to use as little energy to do anything as possible. While this is a necessary survival facet of the brain in early human development, it does not serve the peak performance we are striving for.

"Live as if you were to die tomorrow, learn as if you were to live forever" (Mahatma Gandhi).

Reflections

_____

_____

_____

_____

_____

_____

_____

_____

_____

_____

_____

20

Incorporating the Ideal Vacation

"A vacation is what you take when you can
no longer take what you've been taking."
~Earl Wilson

Each year, you generally are allotted a certain amount of vacation days when you can get away. So the question may arise as to whether you take all the days at once or spread them into "mini breaks." The research from a Finnish university followed fifty-four vacationers through the duration of their getaways, measuring the highs and lows of their happiness and satisfaction as their vacations progressed.

The researchers discovered that vacation-related joy didn't continue to climb upward; instead, happiness peaked after eight days away. The study suggests that a perfectly timed vacation may be to take off on a Friday, as the first day never really feels like a vacation as you get settled in and try to unwind. Additionally, the last day of the vacation in this example, a Sunday, may feel like a workday in that you are packing and getting things together to leave or get ready for the workweek. This is why the "week and a bit" duration seems to be the most appealing.

Reflections

_____

_____

_____

_____

_____

_____

_____

_____

_____

_____

_____

21

Utilizing Binaural Beats

What are brain waves? Your brain is made up of billions of brain cells called neurons which use electricity to communicate with each other. The combination of millions of neurons sending signals at once produces a significant amount of electrical activity in the brain. This electrical activity of the brain is commonly known as a brainwave pattern because of its wave-like nature. You can train your brain to change its brain waves by learning meditation relaxation techniques. However it can take weeks and even years to experience the proven, powerful benefits of brainwave entrainment through meditation alone. A shortcut to getting the best from your brain waves uses the audio tone known as binaural beats.

A binaural beat is an auditory illusion when two different pure-tone sine waves, both with frequencies lower than 1500 hertz and with less than 40 hertz between them, are presented to a listener dichotically (one through each ear). Even through a search of Wikipedia, you can experience an example of binaural beats.

The tendency of the brain to fall in step with a presented stimulus is called "entrainment," and binaural beats are by far the most popular way to train the brain. The benefits of binaural beats are as follows:

- Time alone
- Relaxation

- Better sleep
- Deep meditation
- Positive thoughts
- Heightened mental abilities
- Higher state of consciousness
- Improved health and healing
- Less stress
- Pain management
- Increased focus
- Increased energy

Reflections

_____

_____

_____

_____

_____

_____

_____

_____

_____

_____

_____

22

Taking Breaks – Where and Why

"There is virtue in work, and there is virtue in rest.
Use both and overlook neither."
~Alan Cohen

Want to get more done? Start taking breaks. Studies show we have a limited capacity for concentrating, and although we may not be practiced in recognizing the symptoms of fatigue, they unavoidably derail our work . No matter how engaged we are in an activity, our brains inevitably tire. And when they do, the symptoms are not necessarily obvious.

The benefits of taking fifteen-minute breaks before (not after) you burn out:

- Increased focus.
- Mitigation of fatigue over the course of a workday.
- Replenishing energy.
- Improved self-control and decision making.
- Fueling productivity and improving creativity.
- Goal reactivation. When you work on a task continuously, it's easy to lose focus and get lost in the details. However, following a fifteen-minute break, picking up where you left off forces you to take a few seconds to think globally about what you are trying to achieve. It's a practice that encourages us to stay mindful of our objectives, which encourages better performance.

Tips for finding the time to step away for fifteen minutes before you are depleted:

- One approach that can help is blocking out a couple of planned fifteen-minute breaks on your calendar, one in the mid-morning and one in the afternoon.
- Find something active you can do with this time, and put it on your calendar. Some examples are taking a walk, stretching while listening to your favorite music, or going for a light snack. (The critical thing is to step away from your computer and desk so that your focus is relaxed and your mind can drift.)
- If it feels challenging to take a break, remind yourself that the human brain was not built for extended focus. We actually expect far more of ourselves than centuries of evolution have designed us to do.

Reflections

_____

_____

_____

_____

_____

_____

_____

_____

_____

_____

_____

23

Essential Oils in the Workday

Throughout history essential oils have been used both medicinally and in sacred ceremonies such as meditation. This means that incorporating essential oils into your daily and nightly routines can have a substantial effect on both your emotional and spiritual well-being and your overall health.

Science has shown that essential oils carry the highest vibration of any measured substance, with each oil vibrating at its own frequency. When one comes into contact with the oil's higher vibrational frequency, it will raise the vibrational frequency of the individual. This is beneficial to the overall balance of mind, body, and spirit.

It has been proven that illness can begin to form in a person whose vibrational frequency has dropped below fifty-eight megahertz and that cancer cells can begin to appear at forty-two megahertz. The practice of using essential oils to raise your vibrational frequency can be a simple matter of working them into your daily routine.

Here are a few ways to use essential oils daily:

- Start your day with an uplifting oil like sacred frank-incense, lavender, or myrrh. Place a few drops in your hand, and rub your hands together to create warmth. Cup your hands loosely around your nose and mouth, and inhale deeply. Repeat a number of times through-out your day as you need a light pick-me-up.

- Diffuse your favorite oil in your office or home space. Diffusing an oil makes it airborne, and as we breathe, we receive the benefits of that particular oil. Many will also kill germs in our direct environment. A few good oils to diffuse are Thieves, Abundance, Lavender, and Citrus.
- Apply topically. Many essential oils can be applied topically to the temples, back of the neck, or pulse points to induce relaxation and calm. The bottoms of your feet are also a great place to apply topically as the practice of reflexology indicates that the different zones of the feet correspond with various parts of the body as well as the aura and energetic field.

Some recommended essential oils for relaxation, focus, clarity, and even relief from headache are:

- Lemon: promotes concentration, has a calming effect, and promotes clarity. Lemon also has antiviral and antibacterial properties and can help boost the body's immune system and improve circulation.
- Lavender: helps control emotional stress, promotes calmness, has a soothing effect on nerves, and can relieve nervous tension and uplift spirits as well as ease head tension.
- Jasmine: used to calm nerves, it has an uplifting effect that can help produce a feeling of confidence, optimism, and revitalized energy.
- Rosemary: helps improve memory retention and has stimulating properties that combat physical exhaustion, headaches, and mental fatigue. This can also be used topically to relieve muscular aches and pains.
- Peppermint. Excellent for brainstorming. Boosts energy, invigorates the mind, promotes concentration,

and stimulates clear thinking. Can be applied topically to help reduce muscle fatigue and stress tension in the temples and to increase overall alertness.

Reflections

_____

_____

_____

_____

_____

_____

_____

_____

_____

_____

_____

24

Dressing for Success

"Know first who you are;
then dress accordingly."
~Euripides

What you wear can influence your thinking, negotiation skills, and even hormone levels and heart rate. Many studies show that the clothes you wear can affect your mental and physical performance. Although many of the findings are from small studies in the laboratory, a growing body of research suggests something biological happens when we dress.

- A paper in August 2015 in *Social Psychological and Personality Science* found that wearing formal business attire increased abstract thinking, an important aspect of creativity and long-term strategizing.
- In a study reported in December 2014 in the *Journal of Experimental Psychology*, it was discovered that those who dressed up obtained better results in negotiations including more profitable deals, and those who dressed down had lower testosterone levels.
- In research published in July 2012 in the *Journal of Experimental Social Psychology*, those dressed in professional uniforms such as a lab coat performed better at attention-demanding tasks and made half as many mistakes as when wearing everyday clothes.

- An article in the February 2014 *Journal of Sport and Exercise Psychology* compared the wearing of red versus blue, and concluded that those wearing red were able to lift heavier weight.
- The Red Sneakers Effect: a series of studies published in an article in June 2014 in the *Journal of Consumer Research* explored observer's reactions to people who broke established norms only slightly. For example, a man at a black tie affair was viewed as having a higher status and confidence when wearing a red bow tie. The results suggests that people judge slight deviations from the norm as positive because they suggest that the individual is powerful enough to risk the social costs of such behavior.

Reflections

_____

_____

_____

_____

_____

_____

_____

_____

_____

_____

25

Incorporating Hobbies

"A hobby a day keeps the doldrums away!"
~Phyllis McGinley

Seven benefits of having a hobby:

1. Hobbies encourage taking a break.
2. Hobbies promote eustress – the positive kind of stress, the kind that makes you feel excited about life and what you are doing. Hobbies are one of the best ways to access eustress.
3. Hobbies offer a new challenge. Hobbies break up routine and challenge you in ways that are different from those at work, in avenues that are positive. A new hobby can provide an outlet for challenging yourself without the negative stress that comes with a work-related challenge.
4. Hobbies unite you with others.
5. Hobbies provide an outlet for stress. By focusing on a non-work related task, you are giving your mind something else to focus on.
6. Hobbies promote staying present. If you really love what you are doing, you tend to get in the "flow" or "zone" and truly focus on the moment.
7. Hobbies have physical health benefits. Research has found that engaging in hobbies during downtime is

associated with lower blood pressure, total cortisol, waist circumference, and body mass index. They were also correlated with lower levels of depression.

Reflections

_____

_____

_____

_____

_____

_____

_____

_____

_____

_____

_____

_____

26

Increasing Emotional Intelligence

"When awareness is brought to an emotion,
power is brought to your life."
~Tara Meyer Robson

Emotional intelligence (EQ or EI) can be defined as the ability to understand, manage, and effectively express one's own feelings, as well as engage and successfully navigate the feelings of others. Our EQ can evolve and increase with our desire to learn and grow, unlike IQ which does not change significantly over a lifetime. Here are six basic keys to increasing your emotional intelligence:

1. The ability to reduce negative emotions. Emotional intelligence is extremely important to our ability to effectively manage our own negative emotions so they don't overwhelm us and affect our judgment. To practice this, we must work to change the way we feel about a situation by first changing the way we think about it.

2. The ability to manage stress. When under pressure, the most important thing to keep in mind is to keep our cool.

3. The ability to be assertive and express difficult emotions when necessary. At times it becomes important to communicate our boundaries appropriately so that

101

people know where we stand. One method to consider when needing to express difficult emotion is the XYZ technique – "I feel X when you do Y in situation Z." Avoid using sentences that begin with "you" and are followed by an accusation or judgment.

4. The ability to stay proactive and not reactive in the face of a difficult person. For example, take a time out or slowly count to ten when you feel angry or upset with someone so you can speak from a more centered, calm place. One other way to reduce reactivity is to envision yourself in the difficult person's position, if even for just a moment. By depersonalizing the situation, we can view the situation more objectively and come up with a solution for the problem.

5. The ability to bounce back from adversity. Our choice of how we think, feel, and act in relation to life's challenges makes the difference between hope and despair. Ask questions such as: "What is the life lesson here?" or "How can I learn from this experience?"

6. The ability to express intimate emotions in close personal relationships. The ability to express effectively and validate intimate, loving emotions is essential to maintaining close personal relationships.

Reflections

_____

_____

_____

_____

_____

_____

_____

_____

_____

_____

_____

27

The Benefits of Seeking Coaching

"No problem can be solved by the
same level of consciousness that created it."
~Albert Einstein

Hiring a coach can enhance your personal and professional life. A basic definition of a "life coach" is that he/she helps people move forward and set goals that will give them the life they really want. Most coaching clients are healthy, successful people who might be a little stuck or want to make big changes in their lives. A coach offers support and ample opportunity for deeper self-reflection and accountability.

Coaching can benefit you in the following ways:

- Coaches help you identify and focus on what's important, which can accelerate your insight and success.
- Coaches create a safe environment in which people are often able to see themselves more clearly.
- Coaches identify gaps between where the client is and where the client needs or wants to be.
- Coaches ask for more intentional thought, action, and behavior changes than the client might have asked of himself or herself.
- Coaches guide the building of the structure, accountability, and support necessary to ensure sustained commitment.

- Coaches can help you identify blind spots. This may help you figure out what you don't know and clue you into things you may not be able to see. However, it must be noted that the client alone chooses the specific outcome.
- Coaches help you identify and align with your core values, create focus, and cut through clutter, thereby increasing personal and professional fulfillment.

Reflections

_____

_____

_____

_____

_____

_____

_____

_____

_____

_____

28

The Three R's of Habit Change

"Chains of habit are too light to be felt
until they are too heavy to be broken."
~Warren Buffett

What you do repeatedly ultimately forms the person you are, the things you believe, and the personality that you portray. On this subject, we explore James Clear's strategies to form new habits.

Every habit you have—good or bad—follows the same three-step pattern.

1. Reminder: the trigger that initiates the behavior.
2. Routine: the behavior itself, the action you take.
3. Reward: the benefit you gain from doing the behavior.

To form a new habit, follow these steps:

1. Set a reminder for your new habit. A good reminder does not rely on motivation and it does not require you to remember to do your new habit. A good reminder makes it easy to start by encoding your new behavior in something that you already do. For example, if you want to make flossing your teeth a habit, buy a bowl, place it next to the toothbrush, and put a handful of pre-made flossers in it. In this way, setting

up a physical reminder and linking the new habit with the current behavior makes it much easier to change.

2. Choose a habit that is incredibly easy to start. Don't get caught up in the desire to make massive changes in your life when you are trying to build habits. So here is your action step: decide what you want your new habit to be. Now ask yourself, "How can I make this new behavior so easy to do that I can't say no?"

3. What is your reward? It is important to celebrate. We all want to continue doing things that make us feel good. And because an action must be repeated for it to become a habit, recognizing and rewarding yourself each time you practice your new habit are important.

Reflections

_____

_____

_____

_____

_____

_____

_____

_____

_____

_____

29

Sleep Strategies for Peak Performance

"Each night when I go to sleep, I die. And the
next morning when I wake up, I am reborn."
~Mahatma Gandhi

Sleep studies continually show that the failure to obtain
adequate and consistent, restful sleep is associated with
attention deficits, memory problems, food disturbances, and
impaired mental performance. In fact, chronic sleep loss of
two to four hours per day for two weeks has been found to
degrade performance to the same extent as twenty-four to
forty-eight hours of total sleep deprivation. Unfortunately, 40
percent of all Americans get less than the recommended seven
hours of sleep per night.

- Stick to a consistent wake-up and bedtime every day
  of the week.
- Use the bedroom only for sleep and sex. Professionals
  need to be particularly wary of using technology dev-
  ices within an hour of going to bed. Bottom line: sleep
  and technology in the bedroom don't mix.
- Resolve daily dilemmas outside the bedroom so the
  bedroom retains a sense of rest. A strategy for this is
  to make a "worry list" before going to bed and write
  a brief action item beside each concern. This will allow you a sense of closure each night.

- Establish a bedtime routine. Note: if your bedtime practices have involved practices not conducive to sleep, take some time to break these connections and reestablish a bedtime routine.
- Create a quiet and comfortable sleep environment. A quiet, cool (around 67°F is best), dark, and comfortable environment is crucial for the best possible sleep.
- Don't be a clock watcher. Watching the clock sets up a maladaptive pattern of thinking or worrying about sleep. Knowing what time it is will not improve the quality of sleep, it will not make it easier to go back to sleep, and it will not increase the amount of available sleep time. If necessary, place your clock on a table that is out of reach and facing away from you.
- Don't use alcohol as a sleep aid. The problem with alcohol is that it disrupts the foundational structure of sleep, particularly during the second part of the night. The negative impact of alcohol on sleep quality combined with the effects on the next day's sugar levels makes it a bad choice for anyone seeking optimal performance.

Reflections

_____

_____

_____

_____

_____

_____

_____

_____

_____

_____

_____

_____

30

The Secret to a Fulfilling Life

> "Distance is a bad excuse for not having a good
> relationship with somebody. It's the determination
> to keep it going or let it fall by the wayside;
> that's the real reason that relationships continue."
> ~James McAvoy

A seventy-five-year Harvard study found the number-one secret to leading a fulfilling life. The conclusion? According to Robert Waldinger, director of the Harvard study of adult development, one thing surpasses all the rest in terms of importance: "The clearest message we get from the seventy-five-year study is this; good relationships keep you happier and healthier. Period."

Specifically, the study demonstrates that having someone to rely on helps your nervous system relax, helps your brain stay healthier for longer, and reduces both emotional as well as physical pain. "It's not just the number of friends you have, and it's not whether you're in a committed relationship," says Waldinger. "It's the quality of your close relationships that matters."

These factors include, for example, how much vulnerability and depth exists within them, how safe you feel sharing with one another, and the extent to which you can relax and be seen for who you truly are and truly see another. This is a very good reminder to prioritize not only connection but also your own capacity to process emotions and stress. Take your personal growth seriously so you are available for healthy connection.

Reflections

_____

_____

_____

_____

_____

_____

_____

_____

_____

_____

31

Foods to Increase Focus and Memory

"Tell me what you eat,
and I will tell you who you are."
~Brillet–Savarin

Food and brain performance are inextricably linked. The following fifteen are considered "brain food," according to Dr. Joseph Axe.

1. Avocados
2. Beets
3. Blueberries
4. Bone broth
5. Broccoli
6. Celery
7. Coconut oil
8. Dark chocolate
9. Egg yolks
10. Extra-virgin olive oil
11. Green, leafy vegetables
12. Rosemary
13. Salmon
14. Turmeric
15. Walnuts

Reflections

_____

_____

_____

_____

_____

_____

_____

_____

_____

_____

_____

32

Talking to Yourself Helps You Learn

"Via self-talk we give our mind instructions on
what we expect of ourselves and so behave
accordingly. Change the instructions, and
we change the outcomes."
~Sam Owen

Self-talk (out loud) helps us think about our thinking. When we're engaged in a conversation with ourselves, we typically ask ourselves questions along the lines of: "How will I know what I know?" "What do I find confusing?" "Do I really know this?"

One of the benefits of self-explaining is that it helps people see new links and associations. Seeing these connections helps us improve memory.

Summarizing is a very simple way to engage in self-explaining, since the act of putting an idea into our own words can promote our own learning. For example, by reciting detailed instructions, you will have taken the steps to summarize that knowledge, and you will be far more likely to remember the information.

Reflections

_____

_____

_____

_____

_____

_____

_____

_____

_____

_____

_____

_____

33

Visualization Affirms Your Outcomes

"Visualization is dreaming with purpose."
~Bo Bennett

A practice of visualizing your goals as already complete can rapidly accelerate your achievement of those goals. Jack Canfield writes about four accomplishments that stem directly from utilizing visualization techniques to focus on your goals and desires.

1. It activates your creative subconscious, which will start generating creative ideas to achieve your goal.
2. It programs your brain to more readily garner the resources you need to achieve your goals.
3. It activates a personal energy field, thereby drawing appropriate people and circumstances to you in order to achieve your goals.
4. It helps sustain your motivation to take the steps to achieve your goals.

A sample of techniques to enhance your ability to utilize visualization is as follows:

Technique #1 – A mental rehearsal technique – All one needs to do is to set aside a few minutes a day and practice the following three steps:

A. Sit quietly and imagine you are watching a movie of yourself doing perfectly whatever it is you want to achieve. See as much detail as you can create and recreate in your body any feelings you would wish to be experiencing as you engage in the activities related to your goals.

B. Practice what is called an "embodied image" as if you have actually entered your own visualization and are experiencing things from inside yourself. This will deepen the impact of the experience.

C. Imagine all of your cells are lit up with a movie of you performing perfectly; in other words, internalize and embody what you have visualized.

Technique #2 – Utilize index cards – write each goal on an index card and each morning and night go through the stack of cards, read the goal, close your eyes, and visualize the completion of that goal in its perfect desired state for about fifteen seconds for each card.

Technique #3 – Utilizing affirmations to support your visual – an affirmation is a statement that invokes an experience of already having what you want. Example: I am happily working just four days a week, owning my own business, and traveling readily.

Reflections

_____

_____

_____

_____

_____

_____

_____

_____

_____

_____

_____

34

Identifying Your Values

"When your values are clear to you,
making decisions becomes easier."
~Roy E. Disney

By having a good understand of our values, we can gain tremendous insight, clarity, and focus, which help us to make decisions about priorities and take actions that are aligned with who we most want to be.

There are at least two reasons that values and priorities are important in our lives.

- They enable us to make decisions as to what "best" means to us. For example, the best way to go about something or the right way to do something narrows our choices.
- It affords greater consistency in our lives. In order not to fall into the trap of living by different priorities every day, we become conscious of our values and use them to set priorities to help us stick to a clear and consistent course.

How to go about assessing your values:

- Collect a list of fifteen values that are most important to you in life and business and prioritize them.

- Pay particular attention to the ones that you think are important but are not particularly part of who you are right now.
- Question: Are you consistently living your values in life and business?
- If you are not consistently living your values, question why not and develop insight into what needs to change in order to make that happen.

Reflections

_____

_____

_____

_____

_____

_____

_____

_____

_____

_____

_____

35

Communication Skills for Life

"The single biggest problem in communication
is the illusion that it has taken place."
~George Bernard Shaw

I offer the top ten communication skills for success in work and life.

1. Practice active listening. Active listening involves paying close attention to what the other person is saying, asking clarifying questions, and rephrasing what the other person says to ensure understanding.
2. Be mindful of your nonverbal communication. Your body language, eye contact, hand gestures, and tone all affect the message you are trying to communicate. In addition, pay attention to the other person's nonverbal signals while you are talking, as it is often a clue as to how a person is really feeling.
3. Make sure your communication is clear and concise. Always try to convey your message in as few words as possible; say what you want clearly and directly. Thinking before you speak is a good way to avoid talking excessively or allowing your speech to become confusing.
4. Be mindful of your tone. A friendly, polite tone will always encourage others to engage in more open and

honest communication with you. Additionally, personalizing communication when it is in writing (such as emails) will usually make a recipient feel more appreciated.

5. It is important to be competent in your interaction with others. Exuding confidence can be as simple as making eye contact or using a firm but friendly tone. Confidence helps reassure others that you believe in and will follow through with what you are saying.

6. Demonstrate empathy to show that you understand and respect the other's point of view. This can be as simple as stating, "I understand where you are coming from."

7. Keep an open mind during all conversations so that you can understand the other person's point of view rather than simply getting your own message across. By doing this, you will create an environment for a dialogue even with people who can be disagreeing.

8. Always convey respect for other people and their ideas during communication. Some actions that facilitate another's feeling respected are using a person's name, making eye contact, avoiding distractions, and staying focused on the conversation.

9. It is important to be able to give and receive feedback appropriately. Giving feedback can be as simple as saying "Good job!" or "Thank you!" When accepting feedback, listen carefully, ask clarifying questions, and make efforts to implement the feedback.

10. Choose carefully whether to express something verbally or in writing. As may be obvious, some serious conversations are almost always best done in person.

Reflections

_____

_____

_____

_____

_____

_____

_____

_____

_____

_____

_____

36

Overcoming Negative Thinking

"A positive attitude causes a chain reaction of positive thoughts, events and outcomes. It is a catalyst and it sparks extraordinary results."
~Wade Boggs

As negativity unnecessarily depletes our internal resources, here are ten tips to overcoming negative thoughts:

1. Meditate or do yoga. Meditation and yoga will take the focus from your thoughts and bring attention to the breath. This can increase relaxation and presence to the experience of the moment.
2. Smile! While it actually takes fewer muscles to smile than to frown, it really does help to change your mood and relieve stress.
3. Surround yourself with positive people. When you are stuck in what feels like a negative spiral, turn to the people who can help put things into perspective and won't feed your negative thinking.
4. Change the tone of your thoughts to being solution-oriented.
5. Don't play the victim. You can create your life by taking personal responsibility for your circumstances and acting and thinking accordingly.
6. Volunteer or help someone. To take the focus away

from your own circumstances, helping someone else will automatically make you feel better.

7. Don't get caught in perfectionism. It is easy to dwell on mistakes, but the important thing is to learn from them and let yourself move forward.

8. Sing. When we sing, it often invokes feelings of joy and allows us to show our feelings. This provides amazing stress relief.

9. List five things that you are grateful for right now.

10. Read positive quotes. You may try placing positive quotes on your computer, desk, or mirror as reminders to stay positive.

Reflections

_____

_____

_____

_____

_____

_____

_____

_____

_____

_____

_____

37

Theta Meditation Benefits

Theta meditation produces brain waves of a very low frequency. Theta waves are very close to the delta brain waves which are the lowest frequency that you can achieve and produce a state of deep sleep. When you are in theta meditation, your brain waves produce an extreme state of relaxation.

Theta brain waves appear most often in children and artists as well as people who have spent many years practicing meditation. Theta waves in your brain can help produce intuition, creativity, and strong emotional connections, as well as lower your stress and anxiety.

There are three main avenues that help to achieve theta brain waves:

- Yoga – Yoga is well known for being effective in helping to achieve alpha waves and theta waves. Generally, it will take a great deal of time, practice, patience, and discipline to experience theta brain waves with yoga.
- Meditation – Again, although it may take an extreme amount of practice and dedication, meditation can help increase theta brain waves.
- Brain wave entrainment – You can experience theta meditation by listening to either Mp3 downloads or CDs to provide the frequencies needed to get the brain

to produce the specific brain wave frequency that you desire. These products use binaural beats, monaural beats, or isochronic tones.

Reflections

_____

_____

_____

_____

_____

_____

_____

_____

_____

_____

_____

38

Time Management Tips

"The most successful work smart not hard."
~Bangambiki Habyarimana

There are innumerable tips to manage your time effectively. These are a few tips that many find helpful, though they pose different styles. Allow this list to be a catalyst to get you thinking about how to refine your own practices.

- Complete the most important task first. Each day, identify the two or three tasks that are the most crucial to complete, and do those first.
- Learn to say, "No." At some point, we need to learn to decline opportunities since our objective should be to take on only those commitments that we know we have time for and that we truly care about.
- Devote your entire focus to the task at hand.
- Delineate a time limit in which to complete a task. The time constraint will push you to focus and to be more efficient.
- Leave a buffer—time between tasks. Rushing from task to task makes it challenging to appreciate what we are doing and to stay focused and motivated.
- Don't think of the totality of your to-do list. One of the fastest ways to overwhelm yourself is to dwell on your entire list. Focus on a single task and breathe.

- Lock yourself in. At times the only way to get something done is to keep yourself alone in a room and concentrate without distraction or excuses.
- Eliminate the nonessential. Since our lives are so full of excess, it is important to identify that excess and remove it so that we become more and more in touch with what is significant and deserves our time.
- Find time for stillness. Discovering time in your life for silence and non-motion helps you to remember there is no need to rush constantly.
- Do something during waiting time. Whether it's waiting rooms, standing in line, or using the elliptical at the gym, this is a great time to organize your thoughts or catch up on your reading, as just some examples.

Reflections

_____

_____

_____

_____

_____

_____

_____

_____

_____

_____

_____

39

Personal Responsibility

"In the long run, we shape our lives, and we
shape ourselves. The process never ends until
we die. And the choices we make are
ultimately our own responsibility."
~Eleanor Roosevelt

A person with a winner's mind-set will actually own up and
take responsibility for both things that go right and things
that go wrong. Being responsible means that you will own up
regardless of the outcome. There are two important things to
understand about taking responsibility:

- Avoid attributing blame. When we attribute blame,
  we are usually looking for a scapegoat rather than
  looking for a solution. Being responsible is about
  accepting responsibility for your part in a sequence of
  events and looking for a way forward.
- Being responsible means being positive and solution-
  focused.

When you start being responsible for your outcomes,
you will experience a range of benefits, as follows:

- You become more competent. Taking responsibility
  means that you have the power to make things better.

- You can solve more problems. It is more difficult to solve any problems that arise when you are not focusing on your responsibility. While there are a number of potential causes of any problem, considering your own responsibility will very often lead you to the most likely cause of the problems you experience—you; in other words, your actions or failure to take action.
- You experience better relationships. When someone owns his or her mistake, we can see a little of ourselves in that person. This makes us more likely to react with empathy and compassion, which helps people bond and relate to each other.
- You become a role model. Rather than telling others how they should behave, you begin by demonstrating it by being a suitable role model.
- Improved decision making. By actually taking action and doing something, you are being responsible as opposed to putting off making particular decisions out of fear or worry.

Reflections

_____

_____

_____

_____

_____

_____

_____

_____

_____

_____

_____

40

How to Enter the Flow State

> "Control of consciousness
> determines the quality of life."
> ~Mihaly Csikszentmihalyi

The state of flow or being "in the zone" is a state of peak performance. Those performing in this state often describe it as an ecstatic state to such a point that they may feel as though they almost don't exist. For example, if you were a composer, your hand might seem devoid of itself and the music seems to just flow out of itself.

Positive psychologists—and most notably Dr. Mihaly Csikszentmihalyi, Ph.D.—contend that achieving the flow state on a regular basis is a key component to happiness. More specifically, by learning how to enter the state of flow you can increase your productivity, be more creative, and be happier all at the same time. How to achieve the flow state:

- Find a challenge. Choose something that you enjoy doing.
- Develop your skills in order to be able to meet the challenge. If something is too easy, you won't achieve the flow state because your mind is likely to wander. If something is too hard, you won't be able to achieve that subconscious confidence that is necessary for the flow state.

- Set clear goals. You need to be very clear on what you need to achieve and how you will know whether you are succeeding.
- Focus completely on the task at hand. It is necessary to eliminate all distractions. If your concentration is broken, you are going to exit the state of flow.
- Make sure that you set aside sufficient time. It is very likely that it may take at least fifteen minutes to get into the flow state and a bit longer until you are fully immersed. You will want to make the most of the flow state once you enter it.
- Monitor your emotional state. If you've met all of the requirements above but you are still having trouble entering the flow state, you will need to consider if you are in an inappropriate emotional state (for example: angry, anxious, worried, or low energy). If you can't shake off these emotional states, then try to enter the flow state at a later time.

How does it feel to be in the flow?

- You are completely focused and concentrated on what you are doing.
- You experience a sense of ecstasy, of being outside your everyday reality.
- There is great inner clarity.
- You know the activity is achievable based upon your skills.
- There's an intrinsic motivation; whatever produces flow becomes its own reward.

Reflections

_____

_____

_____

_____

_____

_____

_____

_____

_____

_____

_____

41
Building Great Relationships at Work

"Shared joy is a double joy;
shared sorrow is half a sorrow."
~Swedish proverb

Building and maintaining good working relationships will make you more engaged and committed to your organization, and having a relationship network can also open doors to key projects and career advancement. Devote some portion of your day to laying the foundation of good relationships. The more you give in your relationships, the more you get back from those around you.

How to build good work relationships:

- Develop your people skills. Such skills include collaboration, active listening, communication, and conflict resolution.
- Identify your relationship needs. Know what you need from others and try to understand what they will need from you.
- Schedule time to build relationships. Develop a habit of even short face-to-face interactions to help build the foundation of a good relationship.
- Focus on your emotional intelligence. This is critical to your ability to recognize your own emotions and to understand clearly what they tell you. Additionally,

high emotional intelligence helps you understand the emotional needs of others.

- Appreciate others. Genuinely compliment the people around you when they do something well.
- Be positive. Positivity is attractive and contagious.
- Manage your boundaries. Be aware of how much time you can actually devote during the work day for social interactions, and don't overdo it.
- Avoid gossiping. Talk to people directly about any challenges so as to avoid any mistrust and animosity.
- Listen actively. People respond to those who truly listen, and sincere attention fosters trust.

Reflections

_____

_____

_____

_____

_____

_____

_____

_____

_____

_____

_____

42

Steps to Deal with Difficult Emotions

> "Negative emotions like loneliness, envy
> and guilt have an important role to play in
> a happy life; they're big, flashing signs
> that something needs to change."
> ~Gretchen Rubin

Practicing mindfulness enables you to calm down and to soothe yourself. Following these six steps will help you to understand and deal with your difficult emotions in a mindful way. (These steps come from the Gottman Institute.)

1. Turn toward your emotions with acceptance. The key here is not to push the emotion away. You can sit with anger, anxiety, depression, grief, guilt, sadness, shame, or whatever emotion you are experiencing. Listen to your difficult emotions. They are trying to help you awaken to what is going on before a major crisis occurs.
2. Identify and label the emotion. Instead of saying, "I am angry," say, "This is anger." Acknowledging the presence of emotion empowers you to remain able to just "be" with it. This will allow you to stay present and keep a more objective perception of the emotion.
3. Accept your emotions. Don't deny an emotion. Through mindful acceptance, you can embrace the

difficult feelings with compassion, awareness, and understanding toward yourself and others. You will come to realize that you are not your anger, fear, grief, or any other difficult emotion that you are feeling. Instead, you will begin to experience emotions as if they were clouds that pass by in the sky.

4. Realize the impermanence of your emotions. Allow yourself to witness and observe your emotions with kind attention and patience, giving them the ability to change and in many cases completely evaporate.

5. Inquire and investigate. After you have soothed yourself from the impact of a challenging emotion, take a moment to delve deeply and explore what happened. Asking yourself critical questions, such as looking at the cause or trigger, will help you gain empathy and insight into what you are experiencing.

6. Let go of the need to control your emotions. Be open to the outcome and what unfolds. This will enable you to gain an in-depth understanding of your emotions and your actions surrounding them.

Reflections

_____

_____

_____

_____

_____

_____

_____

_____

_____

_____

_____

43

Is This a Response or a Reaction?

"When you react, you let others control you.
When you respond, you are in control."
~Bohdi Sanders

If mindfulness is being more centered within and aware of others, this is a practice one needs to embrace to prevent reacting and to focus on responding. In terms of a reaction, we often let emotions without reason drive us forward. Responding, however, is more thoughtful and guided more by logic.

Four steps help us respond in a more mindful way:

- Breathing. By focusing on our breathing, we bring our thinking under control and regain concentration.
- Awareness of the body. As we become more aware of our body, it is much easier to bring the body into a steady state and to calm our nervous systems.
- Releasing tension. With each breath and raised awareness, we bring ourselves under control and release tensions. We then can become more centered in who we are and want to be.
- Raising attentiveness. As we maintain inner calmness and strength, we listen more intently and become more aware as we formulate our response. As such, we are able to respond more thoughtfully and engage in more productive areas of discussion.

Reflections

_____

_____

_____

_____

_____

_____

_____

_____

_____

_____

44

Your Locus of Control

"You may not control all the events
that happen to you, but you can decide
not to be reduced by them."
~Maya Angelou

Locus of control as a principle was originated by Julian Rotter in 1954. It considers the tendency of people to believe that control resides internally within them or externally with others or the situation. If you want yourself or others to take more control of their lives, act in a more healthy way, or become more successful at studies or work, encouraging the taking of a more internal position may be helpful.

Internal Locus of Control

People with a high internal locus of control believe in their own ability to control themselves and influence the world around them. They see their future as being in their own hands and that their own choices lead to success or failure. The benefits are as follows:

- It builds confidence.
- People tend to seek information that will help them influence people and situations.
- They will be more motivated and success-oriented.

- They tend to be more specific, generalizing less and considering each situation as unique.

External Locus of Control

People with a high external locus of control believe that control over events and what other people do is outside them and that they personally have little control over such things. The pitfalls of an external locus of control are:

- People tend to be fatalistic, seeing things as happening to them and there is little they can do about it.
- This tends to make people more passive.
- When they succeed, they are more likely to attribute this to luck than their own efforts.

Reflections

_____

_____

_____

_____

_____

_____

_____

_____

_____

_____

_____

45

Complex Problem Solving

"As you sow in your subconscious mind,
so shall you reap in your body and environment."
~Joseph Murphy

Maybe you have noticed that taking some distance from a problem will give you more clarity. Researchers have discovered that a quiet mind allows the connections of non-conscious processing to rise to awareness.

Neuroscientist David Creswell explored what happens in the brain when people attempt to solve problems that are too big for their conscious mind. In short, he discovered that people did significantly better when something that lightly held their conscious attention (a distractor) was given but allowed their subconscious to keep working. According to Creswell, the brain regions that were active during the initial, conscious problem solving continued to be active even when the brain was distracted with another task. This is called un-conscious reactivation.

To put it plainly, people who were lightly distracted for a period of time did better on a complex problem-solving task than people who continued to put in conscious effort. Even being distracted for only a few minutes causes this ef-fect because the problem-solving resources of the uncon-scious are millions if not billions times larger than those of the conscious.

Keep in mind, this isn't the "sleep on it" effect or an effort to quiet the mind. This is something accessible to all of us every day, in many small ways. The take-away to this research is to take a "distractor break," even if less than thirty seconds, to have new breakthroughs.

Reflections

_____

_____

_____

_____

_____

_____

_____

_____

_____

_____

_____

46

The Nefarious Power of Negativity

"The brain is like Velcro for negative
experiences but Teflon for positive ones."
~Rick Hanson, Ph.D.

Researchers have concluded that people generally learn faster from pain than pleasure. This is commonly referred to as the "negativity bias." Unfortunately, our brain is more affected by negative than positive information.

Negative events bring about the elements of the fight or flight response; we feel anxious, our pulse increases, our breathing seems to require more effort, and so on. In essence, an automatic vigilance mechanism seems at play here in that negative events attract the brain's attention and exert a greater impact on brain processing than positive events.

What should we do to shift this imbalance?

- Information is power. Once you realize that negative information weighs more heavily on the brain, it is important to actively counter it with a more positive interpretation of events.
- Be mindful of the fact that our brains have evolved in a way that routinely may result in the following three mistakes: overestimating threats, underestimating opportunities, and underestimating resources. To counter this, emphasize reassuring good news and use

tools to counteract anxiety which will be described in more detail in another section.

- When something positive does occur, make a point to savor the experience; literally replay it in your mind over and over so that the memory of the positive experience is stored in your long-term memory.
- Keep a ratio of five to one in your dealings with others. Since others will be more affected by the negative things you say or do, in many instances you will need to do or say five positive things to maintain a positive relationship.
- Scatter simple pleasures throughout your day. The small doses of positivity will help your brain counteract its natural negativity bias. Gretchen Rubin, owner of "The Happiness Project," recommends that you create an "area of refuge" in your brain. Specifically, have a list of positive things ready; for example, good memories, inspiring quotes, lines from books or movies, anything you can think of whenever you find your mind wandering to a negative memory.

Reflections

_____

_____

_____

_____

_____

_____

_____

_____

_____

_____

_____

47

Meditation Tips for Beginners

"Meditation is listening to the Divine within."
~Edgar Cayce

During meditation, one's metabolism and breath rate drop to a level of rest, twice that of deep sleep. Many people, however, view meditation as unappealing, for it sounds like another thing they don't have time to do. You do not have to meditate for hours to gain the many benefits of meditation.

Here are tips to overcome any challenges you may experience in beginning a meditation practice.

- Start small. Three to five minutes or less is a meaningful beginning. If that still feels like too much, pay attention to three long, deep breaths.
- Remember that meditation is an antidote to stress, anxiety, irritability, or overthinking. Remind yourself that you have the power to calm your own nervous system.
- Understanding the principles of meditation, becoming aware of what you are thinking, is the first step to restructuring your thoughts. Another useful goal in your meditation is to become aware of when your mind has drifted. A useful goal for beginning meditators is the ability to redirect your attention back to your point of focus without criticizing yourself.

- Incorporate informal meditation into your day such as witnessing your own thoughts as they occur, without judgment, or simply paying attention to the sensations of your breathing each time you switch tasks.
- Learn to recognize your own "monkey mind," as Buddhists call it, when your thoughts drift from thing to thing like a monkey swinging from tree to tree.
- Remember that you are not your thoughts. In fact, remind yourself that you do not have to believe every thought you have. This is a valuable step toward living mindfully so we don't squander precious seconds of our lives, as we tend to worry about the future and ruminate about what is past.

Reflections

_____

_____

_____

_____

_____

_____

_____

_____

_____

_____

_____

48

Controlling Anger

"The best fighter is never angry."
~Lao Tzu

Anger is a completely normal, often healthy, human emotion. Obviously, however, when it gets out of control and turns destructive, it can lead to problems. As Ambrose Bierce once said, "Speak when you are angry and you will make the best speech you will ever regret."

Strategies to work with anger:

- Utilize relaxation techniques. This can take the form of deep breathing and relaxing visualization. Breathe deeply, from your diaphragm; breathing from your chest won't relax you. You may also try repeating a calming word or phrase while breathing deeply. It is important to practice the techniques daily so that you learn to use them automatically.
- When you are angry, your thinking can get exaggerated and even overly dramatic. Remind yourself that getting angry is not going to fix anything and that it will actually make you feel worse. Logic defeats anger since anger, even when justified, can quickly become irrational. Be mindful of using words like "never" or "always," and remind yourself that you are just experiencing the normal challenges of everyday life.

- Problem solve. Not all anger is misplaced. It is possible to make a plan and resolve to give your best shot at a solution without punishing yourself if an answer doesn't come right away. In extra-challenging situations, it may be most productive to focus not on finding the solution but rather on how you will handle and face the problem.
- Using humor. While it is not productive just to "laugh off" your problems, use humor to help yourself face challenges more constructively. Utilize a mental image you can conjure for a situation that is making you angry to help you see the humor in the situation. The more detail you can get into your imagery scenes, the more chances you have to see that maybe you are being unreasonable or how unimportant the things you are angry about really are. Lastly, a note of caution: don't give in to sarcastic humor as that's just another form of unhealthy anger expression.
- Change your environment. Sometimes your environment and the people around you give you cause for irritation and fury. Make sure you give yourself some personal time for the times of the day that you know are particularly stressful. After a brief quiet time, you will find yourself better prepared to handle challenges without escalating to anger.

Reflections

_____

_____

_____

_____

_____

_____

_____

_____

_____

_____

_____

49

Five Steps to a Clearer Mind

"Believe it or not, at least a third
of your worries should get trashed."
~James Clear

We have all encountered situations during the workday when thoughts from the many areas of life intrude in our minds, which obviously makes it difficult to concentrate on a task. On these occasions, there is a very good chance that you have acquired too many "open loops" in your mind, but you can close those loops and actually get long-lasting relief within the hour.

James Clear teaches a five-step method for getting a clearer mind, which works wonders when done correctly.

The Clear Mind Procedure

1. Write down everything that's on your mind on one piece of paper (or more if you need it).
2. Create three columns on a second piece of paper and label them as follows: To Be Done, Maybe Later, and Delete. Sort all the items on the first piece of paper into the three columns on the second piece of paper.
3. Take each item from the Delete column, send it off into space, and tell it to never return (with a corny little ceremony if that helps).

4. Take the items from the Maybe Later column, and put them on a Maybe Later list. (If you don't already keep one, start one.)
5. Take the items from the To Be Done column, and put them into your planning system. (If you don't have a planning system, get one.)

It is very important for this exercise that you literally write down everything that is on your mind, not just your unfinished tasks. These might include the following:

*   Unfinished tasks
*   Trips or plans you want to make
*   People with whom you should touch base
*   Areas of your life in which you feel inadequate
*   Regrets about past choices
*   Home repair issues
*   Your worries
*   Habits you want to establish or break
*   Things with which you are dissatisfied and want to change.

Realize that all of this "stuff" competes for your attention. If you want a clear mind, you must deal with all of it. In doing this exercise, you may begin to realize how much clutter that you have allowed into your mind. Importantly, you will begin to realize how much of that clutter is things you can't do anything about or at least don't need to do anything about right now.

In doing this exercise, don't be surprised if you get dozens (or even hundreds) of things off your mind!

Reflections

_____

_____

_____

_____

_____

_____

_____

_____

_____

_____

_____

50

Shifting Your Thoughts

"Even the worst circumstance
can be transformed by our minds."
~Viktor Frankl

According to Dr. Robert Holden, "The meaning of life is made, not found." He, like Frankl, outlined some profound tips for us to reconsider the meaning we place on life events. Victor Frankl was a survivor of the Nazi concentration camps, and his horrific experiences taught him that people can survive any hardship if they are able to make a positive meaning out of it. Consider the following as ways to practice shifting your thoughts.

1. The meaning of life is not a search; it is a choice. The world means nothing by itself. You give it all the meaning it has. As Dr. Holden writes, "The meaning of life is a choice you make, not just once, but every waking hour of your day. Life is like art—it is all about interpretation." Whatever meaning you attach to an event, it governs your perception, your thinking, your choices, your feelings, your behavior, everything! Whenever you are able to elect a new meaning, this can change everything.

2. Thought shift is a great key to healing and success. As William Shakespeare wrote, "There is nothing either

good or bad but thinking makes it so." Here are some examples for you to consider:

- Getting fired might mean the end of your life, or a new beginning.
- A boss who spends no time communicating with you—maybe he doesn't value you, or perhaps he trusts you completely.
- A failed job interview might mean that you lost out, or something even better is in store.

As you can see, your interpretation and meaning decide everything after an event.

3. Your ego is an avid interpreter, quick to interpret events as good or bad, or right or wrong. This is especially true during a crisis when judgment and anxiety cloud your mind. Choosing to shift your thoughts can help to suspend the ego's fearmongering. Fear is not in things; fear is only in the meaning you give things. Pain is not in things; pain is only in the meaning you give things. Change the meaning, and the fear and pain are transformed. Meaning is always a choice.

The 180-shift Exercise

- Think of something you would label as wrong, bad, painful, or negative.
- Declare, "This could mean anything."
- Suspend all judgments and clear your mind.
- Be open to a higher inspiration, a new perception, and a more positive interpretation.

Doing the 180-shift exercise with another person can be very beneficial.

Reflections

_____

_____

_____

_____

_____

_____

_____

_____

_____

_____

_____

51

The Benefits of Being in Nature

"In every walk with nature
one receives far more than one seeks."
~John Muir

Recent studies about the effects of walking in nature have been directed at understanding how this activity affects both the physiological and mental aspects of our brains. One of the main reasons for this research is because Americans spend about 93 percent of their time inside a building or a vehicle. The bright side is when it comes to the outdoors, as with all great medicine, a little goes a long way.

- Nature really does clear your head. According to a study published in the *Proceedings of the National Academy of Sciences*, a ninety-minute walk through a natural environment showed positive impacts such as lower levels of brooding or obsessive worry, while the control group who spent ninety minutes walking through a city reported no such difference. Additionally, the brain scans of the subjects revealed decreased blood flow to a region associated with bad moods. In essence, hiking in nature deactivates everything from feeling sad to worrying and even to major depression.
- Unplugging makes you more creative. Psychologists Ruth Ann Atchley and David L. Strayer found in their

2012 study that after a four-day hike in the wilderness, with no access to technology, participants scored 50 percent higher on a test (known as remote Associates Test) which measures creative potential in people. By research standards, this is a huge leap in performance. The study also indicates that our ability to think creatively is being overwhelmed by the constant stimulus of digital, indoor living.

- Charge your mind's battery with a hike. Aerobic exercise has a really positive effect on your brain in that it substantially improves your memory. Outdoor activity has also been shown to improve grades. According to a 2010 report in the *Journal of Environmental Science and Technology*, even getting out into nature for five minutes at a stretch is enough to give your self-esteem a substantial upgrade. Spending the entire day outdoors results in a second jump upwards! Walking near water seemed to have the biggest effect.

What science demonstrates is that walking in nature is a solid choice for making life and mental health better, even with very little effort.

Reflections

52

A Humane Approach to Your Workday

"Working hard and working smart
sometimes can be two different things."
~Byron Dorgan

This section is intended to speak to the most effective structuring of the workday. Taking into account that many professionals are tasked with billing for an hour of time and therefore may feel they have little flexibility, my hope is that this section does empower individuals with information when there is more latitude in terms of the timing of work hours. Studies have shown that the eight-hour workday is actually an ineffective approach to work in terms of productivity and feelings of well-being. In fact, some would argue it is actually holding people back.

A study conducted by the Draugiem Group found that the length of the workday did not increase productivity levels, but what really mattered was how people structured their day. Specifically, individuals taking short breaks were far more productive than those who worked longer hours.

The Best Way to Structure Your Day

According to science, the ideal work-to-break ratio is fifty-two minutes of work followed by seventeen minutes of rest. Maintaining this ratio helps people maintain a unique level of focus in their work. The human brain naturally functions in spurts of high energy (roughly an hour followed by spurts of low energy of fifteen to twenty minutes).

How to Beat Exhaustion and Distractions at Work

Intentionality about your workday is the key to productivity along with being aware of your body when your energy starts to ebb and flow. It is important to schedule *real breaks*, as checking email or other social media does not recharge you the same way as taking a walk does.

What's clear from the research is that even if you find yourself needing to put in a significant number of hours per day, if you intentionally structure the hours that are worked and infuse your day with real self-care, you will find yourself more productive and effective.

Reflections

_____

_____

_____

_____

_____

_____

_____

_____

_____

_____

_____

53

Cultivating Self-compassion

"If your compassion does not include yourself,
it is incomplete."
~Jack Kornfield

Self-compassion, otherwise known as self-love, is a construct drawn from Buddhist psychology and refers to relating to the self with kindness. Psychologist Kristin Neff defines self-compassion as follows: "Kindness toward the self, which entails being gentle, supportive, and understanding as opposed to harshly judging one's self. Self-compassion should be offered to ourselves in the form of warmth and unconditional acceptance, even when we make mistakes." When you practice self-compassion, you understand that your worth is unconditional.

Why is this important? Research has consistently shown a positive correlation between self-compassion and psychological well-being, greater social connectedness, emotional intelligence, happiness, and overall life satisfaction. It has also been shown to correlate with less anxiety and depression. Additionally, people who lack self-compassion often exhibit a pattern of unhealthy relationships. As author Anis Qizilbash puts it, "How you treat yourself reflects how you let others treat you."

The following are five ways to begin practicing self-compassion:

- Treat yourself as you would a small child.
- Practice mindfulness. Mindfulness helps us to monitor our internal negative self-talk and becomes an antidote to our inner critic and negative rumination.
- Remember that you are not alone. It is important to remind ourselves that not one of us is perfect and that we are all connected. As Dr. Daniel Bover states, "Self-compassion is about being kind to ourselves and realizing that the human condition is imperfect and that our flaws and setbacks should connect us and not divide us."
- Give yourself permission to be imperfect. It may be useful to think of the idea of giving yourself permission to make a mistake as a way of accepting however you are feeling and knowing that other people have also felt this way.
- Work with a supportive therapist or coach. Finding a good therapist or coach can help you to become aware of your own thoughts and feelings, to have a realistic perspective of yourself and others, and to allow you to experience another's empathy for you.

Reflections

_____

_____

_____

_____

_____

_____

_____

_____

_____

_____

_____

54

Developing a Nonjudgmental Attitude

"Mindfulness means paying attention in a
particular way; on purpose, in the present
moment, and non-judgmentally."
~Jon Kabat-Zinn

Kabat-Zinn's definition highlights that an important aspect of mindfulness is avoiding harsh judgments of ourselves and others. Acceptance means we accept our experience with equanimity (being aware of our experience without either clinging to it or pushing it away). It really means that you do not define yourself or measure your validation by the unpleasant emotions you may experience.

The following are two approaches to foster acceptance of our feelings and experiences.

- Locating the feeling within your own body.
  a. What shape is the feeling?
  b. Where exactly is it located?
  c. What color, if any, is it?

In locating the emotion within your body, you come to realize that if you stand back from the emotion, not everything you are experiencing is colored by just one strong emotion. In this way, we are not so prone to get caught up in it.

- Developing a spirit of curiosity. As you learn to identify your emotions, such as in the exercise delineated above, you can recognize that your thoughts are just thoughts and not reality. Thoughts only keep going as long as we put energy into them. An example of an exercise that may be helpful is to say words like: "It's okay. Let me feel this. It's okay to feel this." With this practice, we can replace the aversion we have to the unpleasant feeling and break the vicious cycle by not feeling bad about feeling bad. Additionally, when we name our experience, we also create a small gap that gives us a sense of freedom.

Reflections

_____

_____

_____

_____

_____

_____

_____

_____

_____

_____

_____

_____

55

A Healthy Relationship with Money

"If you want to find the secrets of the universe,
think in terms of energy, frequency and vibration."
~Nikola Tesla

The latest discoveries in quantum physics have proven that everything around us, including us, is made up of pure energy. In fact, as soon as scientists started smashing electrons in enormous accelerators, they found the building blocks of all matter are, in fact, energy.

Whether it is our upbringing, the media, or even the opinions of others, a great deal of external influences are responsible for creating the "story" we tell ourselves about money. Some people have come to believe that money—or the lack of it—is something to be feared. They may even live constantly in the shadow of their money worries. On the other hand, some people remain confident that money comes freely and with ease. To some, it may even appear that these people attract money wherever they go.

The important thing is to recognize that your own financial "story" could be one of the main reasons you are not enjoying the abundance you yearn for. The purpose of this section is to help you examine your experiences and beliefs about money in order to let go of the disempowering beliefs.

Remember, since everything in our lives is made up of energy, it goes without saying that our money, too, is made up of energy. This energy, like everything else, is impacted by the thoughts, words, and emotions we fuel it with.

Here are some of the common limiting beliefs people have about money. Identify what incorrect beliefs you have been holding.

- Money has to be earned the hard way.
- Money is a limited resource.
- Money is the root of all evil.
- Money doesn't come easily to people like me.
- I don't deserve money.
- I can't afford to buy. . . .

Once you've uncovered the limiting beliefs negatively impacting your relationship with money, begin a practice of utilizing more positive, supportive beliefs to overwrite the old, limiting ones.

- I am a magnet for money.
- Prosperity is drawn to me.
- I move from poverty-thinking to abundance-thinking.
- I am worthy of making more money.
- I am open and receptive to all the wealth life wants to offer me.
- Money and spirituality can coexist in harmony.

Reflections

_____

_____

_____

_____

_____

_____

_____

_____

_____

_____

_____

56

Mindfulness with Difficult Emotions

"Rather than letting our negativity get the better
of us, we could acknowledge that right now we
feel like a piece of shit, and not be squeamish
about taking a good look."
~Pema Chordon

All of us can relate to experiencing difficult emotions like anger, confusion, fear, loneliness, and sadness, just to name a few. Unfortunately, emotions like these can feel like the most present and powerful forces in your life. Mindfulness is a key to dealing with these challenging emotions. Practicing mindfulness enables you to slow down and empower yourself with the ability to soothe yourself.

Toni Parker, Ph.D., writes about a powerful six-step process to mindfully deal with difficult emotions. The steps are as follows:

1. Turn toward your emotions with acceptance. The key to this step is to not push any emotion away and certainly not to bottle it up inside. Sit with whatever emotion you are experiencing, become aware of it, and don't ignore it. If you find this difficult, focus on your breath or get up and walk around a bit. It is important to listen to your difficult emotions, as they are often trying to wake you up to what is going on.

2. Identify and label the emotion. Instead of saying, "I am angry" say, "This is anger," or, "This is anxiety." In this way, you are acknowledging the presence of the emotion while empowering yourself to remain detached from it. Labeling a painful experience will allow you to take some pain out of the feeling, which in turn allows you to stay in the present versus catapulting yourself into the future or trapping yourself in the past.

3. Accept your emotions. Acknowledge and accept whatever emotion is present and whatever you are experiencing in that moment. Through mindful acceptance, you can embrace difficult feelings with compassion, awareness, and understanding toward yourself and others. If you have difficulty with this, think of a friend or a loved one who might be having a hard time, and imagine what you would say to them. Say the same thing to yourself.

4. Realize the impermanence of your emotions. Every emotion is impermanent. It is certainly easy to forget this when you are in the midst of dealing with difficult emotions. As Dr. Parker writes, "Allow yourself to witness and observe your emotions with kind attention and patience, giving them the latitude to morph and, in many cases, completely evaporate."

5. Inquire and investigate. After you have calmed yourself from the impact of your emotions, take a moment to explore what triggered the emotion or from where the discomfort arose. Ask yourself critical questions to create space to see things with a new perspective.

6. Let go of the need to control your emotions. The key to dealing mindfully with your difficult emotions is to let go of your need to control them. Instead, be open to the outcome and what unfolds.

Reflections

_____

_____

_____

_____

_____

_____

_____

_____

_____

_____

_____

57

Practices for Boosting Happiness

"People are just as happy
as they make up their minds to be."
~Abraham Lincoln

Positive psychology is the scientific study of the strengths and positive traits that enable individuals and communities to thrive. It is founded on the belief that people want to lead meaningful and fulfilling lives, to accentuate their positive traits, and to enhance their experiences of love, work, and play.

In this section, there will be ten practices to make it easier for you to feel happier. It is best to set aside five to sixty minutes a day to tackle at least one of the steps below.

1. Know that life hurts but happiness is the cure. While happy and unhappy people have the same pain and trauma, the difference is that happy people bounce back more quickly. When you cultivate a happier attitude, you become less dependent on external sources of validation and trust your thoughts, emotions, and behaviors.

2. Start a gratitude journal. When we constantly think about negative events or setbacks, we lose perspective. By keeping a simple journal of what you are grateful for, it helps you to gain the lost perspective.

To do this, write three things daily and refer to your journal when you are feeling down.

3. Add the gratitude diary. The gratitude diary is a practice wherein you highlight how you got from a negative thought to a more positive one. Start by writing from three to five things you liked each day, and ask yourself the following questions: What happened to me? What did I do right? How did I help it to happen? After doing this, write one thing you did not like and ask yourself: How is this keeping me stuck? Then, examine the thoughts and actions that got you unstuck and in a better mood. After repeating this daily, you will begin to see your negative thought patterns, and you can refocus your energy on doing things differently.

4. Practice optimism. When you master the attitude of optimism, you understand that good things are coming and that the bad things pass quickly.

5. Write your future diary. When you see yourself as capable of solving problems, you are more likely to find ways to solve them. Write about your preferred future as follows: What will it look like? What will you feel? How will your life change?

6. Savoring. Savoring positive experiences helps us to appreciate life as we take the time to slow down and become more mindful of what's around us. Choose a ritual wherein you savor one experience each day, and you will soon develop a nice habit.

7. Count kindness gestures. Keep a log of all the kind acts that you do in a particular day.

8. Record three funny things. In doing this, notice why the funny thing happened.

9. "Gift your time." Offer your time to three different people in a week.

10. Gratitude visit. Think of someone you should thank, write a letter to this person, and tell that one how he or she has helped you and how that affected you later. You may then share the letter with your friend. This should benefit your mood and the mood of your friend for many weeks.

Reflections

_____

_____

_____

_____

_____

_____

_____

_____

_____

_____

58

The Many Benefits of Traveling

"The real voyage of discovery consists not in
seeking new landscapes but in having new eyes."
~Marcel Proust

If there is one piece of advice I have for people today to experience more joy in life, it is to travel more. By traveling, I am not referring simply to taking vacations or going on preplanned trips; it means here to go somewhere you have never gone to let life show you what opportunities have been waiting for you that you might not have imagined otherwise. There are many wonderful benefits of traveling, and some even scientifically proven. A few of the many benefits are outlined herein.

Adam Siddiq outlines nine fantastic benefits of traveling (http://www.lifehack.org/author/adamsiddiq), with which I could not agree more.

1. You will find a new purpose. Traveling is an amazingly underrated investment in you. With the newness of discovering new people, cultures, and lifestyles, you are also open to new ways of seeing the world and living, which often gives a renewed sense of purpose in life. This is especially ideal if you are feeling stuck in your career or life. By traveling, you might be surprised to discover a new life purpose and direction.

2. You'll appreciate your home more. Traveling in areas where people do not have the same basic goods and luxuries as we may take for granted will really help us to appreciate what we do have.
3. You will realize your home is more important than just where you grew up. The more we travel, the more we perceive that our "home" is the world itself, and we may become more aware of how we can live harmoniously and support one another.
4. You'll realize how little you actually knew about the world. When we travel, we begin to notice that the world is actually much different than we have been told or indoctrinated to believe. Also, many myths about travel get dispelled, such as that it is either too expensive or dangerous. You may also come to realize how kind and friendly strangers can be, even in areas that are supposedly unwelcoming.
5. You'll realize that we all share similar needs. As you travel, you notice the truth of this even more, and you become more able to relate to people regardless of their background.
6. You'll realize that it is extremely easy to make friends. Something magical happens in how people can show up in a very raw and real state when they are out of their conditioned environment. This rawness helps facilitate quick and strong friendships.
7. You'll experience the interconnectedness of humanity across the world.
8. You'll experience serendipity and synchronicity. "Traveling is one of the easiest ways to become aware of the magic that weaves all of creation together through serendipity and synchronicity, with perfect timing," explains Adam Siddiq.
9. You'll realize life is a wonderful gift. "Twenty years

The Many Benefits of Traveling

from now you will be more disappointed by the things you didn't do than by the things you did do," stated the world traveler, Mark Twain.

As we travel and experience more of the world, we often start perceiving more gratitude and appreciation and become alive with energy.

Reflections

_____

_____

_____

_____

_____

_____

_____

_____

_____

_____

_____

59

Knowing and Finding Your Life Purpose

"Your purpose is your why."
~Deborah Day

We can't really think our way into our life's passion and purpose, and we each have our own expression of this. It will most likely mean taking steps toward what you actually want and removing those things in your life you don't want. Author Shannon Kaiser offers three unique steps to get closer to your purpose and passion:

- Get more action. "You can't think your way into finding your life purpose; you have to do your way into it. Very simply, rather than overthinking it, start trying new things. Clarity will come through the process of exploring, and action is where you get results," says Shannon Kaiser.
- Drop from your head to your heart. Ask yourself what you love, what you have a passion for. Ms. Kaiser explains, "When you are inspired and connected to your happy self, inspiration will flood your heart and soul. When you lead from your heart, you are actually more joyful and motivated to explore."
- Break up with "the one." By trying to find only one thing that we are meant to do, we may end up feeling like something is missing. As Kaiser states, "Let go of

thinking there is only one purpose for you, and embrace the idea that our purpose in life is to love life fully by putting ourselves fully into our life!" In fact, the need to seek our purpose comes mostly from a lack of passion. Kaiser boils it down to a simple equation: passion + daily action = purposeful life.

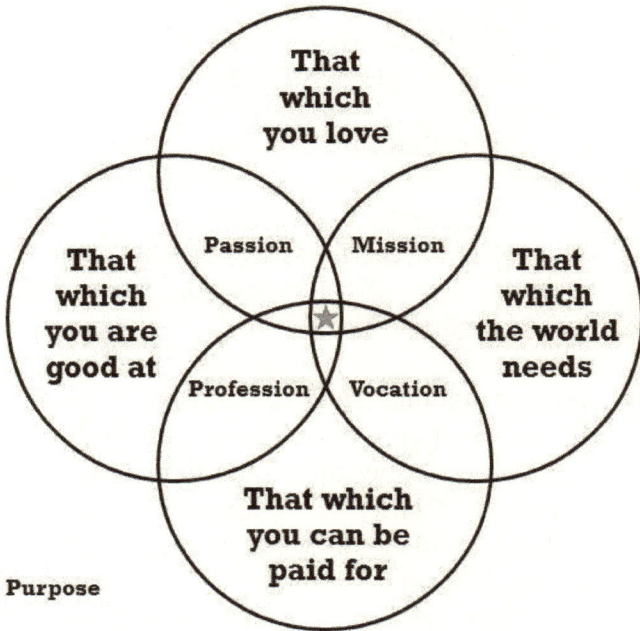

That
which
you love

Passion   Mission

That
which
you are
good at

That
which
the world
needs

Profession   Vocation

★ Purpose

That which
you can be
paid for

Reflections

_____

_____

_____

_____

_____

_____

_____

_____

_____

_____

_____

60

Really Getting to Know Yourself

"Know thyself."
~Plato

Here are a few reasons it is important to really know your own nature. We will refer to these as the benefits of self-knowledge.

- You will be happier when you can express who you are. Also, expressing your desires increases the chance that you will get what you want.
- When your inner feelings and values are congruent with your outside actions, you will experience less inner conflict.
- The more you know yourself, the better able you are to make choices in your life that feel aligned with who you are.
- When you understand what motivates you to exert self-control, you have the insight to know which values and goals motivate you.
- When you are grounded in knowing your values and preferences, you are less likely to say "yes" when you meant to say "no."
- An awareness of your own inner struggles will help you develop more tolerance and empathy toward others.

- Being who you truly are helps you experience greater vitality and pleasure in life.

The Building Blocks of Self-knowledge

- Know your values.
- Know your temperament.
- Know when you like to do things (often referred to as your biorhythms).
- Ask yourself, "What have been the most meaningful events of my life?" You may discover clues to your hidden identity, career, and even life satisfaction.
- Know your strengths and your weaknesses.

Reflections

_____

_____

_____

_____

_____

_____

_____

_____

_____

_____

_____

61

Work–Life Balance: How to Find It

"You will never feel truly satisfied with work
until you are satisfied by life."
~Heather Schuck

Achieving the elusive "work–life balance" can often feel like an impossible goal. Certainly, work–life balance will vary over time. The exercise herein will help you consider the things that compete for your time and reprioritize your life in an intentional way. On the wheel below, rate your level of satisfaction in eight areas of your life. One means not satisfied and ten means highly satisfied.

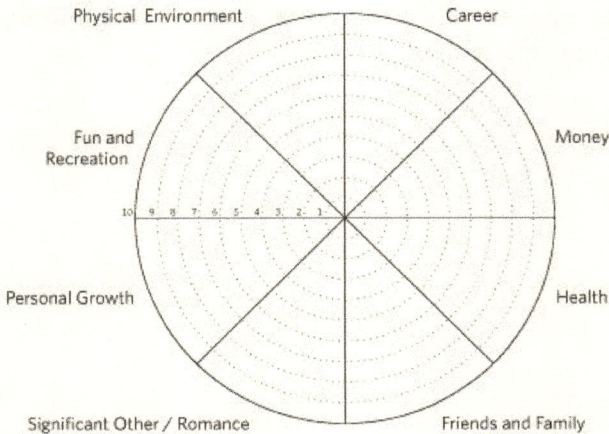

Physical Environment — Career

Fun and Recreation — Money

Personal Growth — Health

Significant Other / Romance — Friends and Family

10 9 8 7 6 5 4 3 2 1

Example:

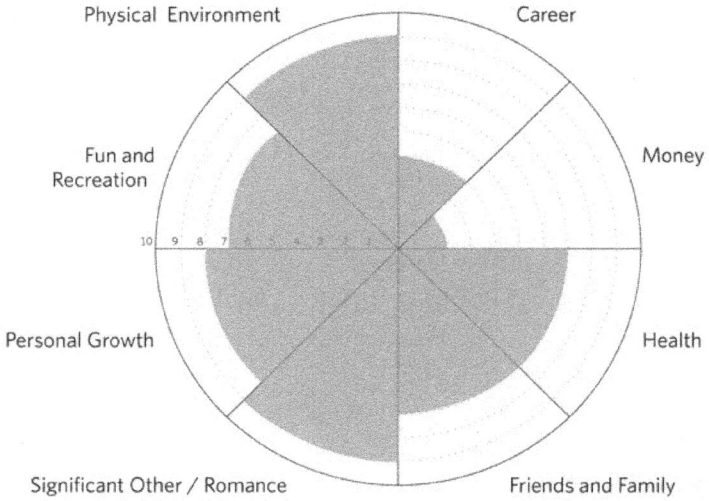

After completing this exercise, you can now mindfully and intentionally create the life that is most congruent with your priorities and passions.

"Balance is not something you find, it is something you create" (Jana Kingsford).

Reflections

_____

_____

_____

_____

_____

_____

_____

_____

_____

_____

_____

_____

62

Intrinsic / Extrinsic Motivation

Motivation is something that energizes, directs, and sustains our behaviors. When it comes to our happiness and fulfillment, that we understand what motivates us is very important. There are two types of motivation.

- Intrinsic Motivation – internal desire to perform a particular task. People do certain activities because it gives them pleasure, develops a particular skill, or is felt to be morally the right thing to do. The intrinsic value of something is said to be the value that the thing has for its own sake.

- Extrinsic Motivation – factors external to the individual and unrelated to the task they are performing. In this case, people act because they seek validation or tangible benefits. Examples include money, recognition, and other rewards.

It has been thought by both philosophers and researchers that intrinsic value is of greater importance to motivation and well-being than extrinsic motivation.

However, Abraham Maslow concluded that before we can be intrinsically motivated, we must first have our more basic human needs met in an established hierarchy. Maslow identified five basic levels of human needs, as follows:

1. Physiological needs. These are needs that ensure our physical survival such as food, water, air, shelter, clothing, and sex. It is important to note whether your physiological needs are being met because only then will you be able to concentrate on higher-level needs.
2. Safety needs. Safety and security needs include order, stability, routine, control over one's life and environment, certainty, and health.
3. Social needs. These needs include love, affection, belonging, and acceptance.
4. Esteem needs. All people have a need for a stable, friendly based, usually high evaluation of themselves or self-respect, self-esteem.
5. The need for self-actualization. This level of hierarchy is concentrated on an individual being able to reach his or her full potential as a human being. Once someone has satisfied the first four levels of needs, that person has the ability to concentrate on functioning to his or her highest potential.

The first four needs are what are referred to as deficiency needs because they come from things we are lacking. These needs can be met only by external sources, by the environment, people, or things going on around us. Self-actualization is a growth need; it gives us room to grow and develop as an individual. This need is always intrinsically motivated, because we do it out of pure enjoyment and desire to grow.

In conclusion, intrinsic motivation will not occur until our basic needs are met. From there intrinsic motivation will come easily.

Reflections

63

Survive and Thrive through Change

"Life is a series of natural and spontaneous changes.
Don't resist them; that only creates sorrow.
Let reality be reality. Let things flow naturally
forward in whatever way they like."
~Lao Tzu

How you deal with changes in your life will determine whether the changes make you happier or reduce you to frustration and distress. Marilyn Tam developed a five-step process to help people deal with each major life change from a place of deeper wisdom. She calls the system "PAGDE," and it can be applied to both your business and your personal life changes.

- *P*ause: take many deep breaths and repeat them until you feel the adrenalin in your body begin to slow. Whatever the impending change, you will always benefit by slowing down and gaining perspective.
- *A*ssess: what are the true dimensions of the issue? Who, what, when, and how? Whether you are initiating the process of change or not, ask the questions with no judgment and an open mind.
- *G*ather: why did this happen? Is this a natural life process? Is this something that was precipitated by an outside circumstance? What are the possible solutions

and the consequences of the various options and action steps?

- **D**ecide: based on the above information, determine the appropriate next steps to resolve the issue and to prevent new ones if applicable. Always keep your life purpose and life values in your consideration.
- **E**xecute: resolve the challenge with commitment and the comfort that you have assessed, analyzed, and come up with the best solution for all concerned.

With change always comes lessons; always give thanks for the lessons of change. Each change is a step in our life journey and also an occasion for growth and increased capacity for joy and compassion.

"I have accepted fear as part of life—specifically then fear of change. . . . I have gone ahead despite the pounding in the heart that says turn back" (Erica Jong).

Reflections

_____

_____

_____

_____

_____

_____

_____

_____

_____

_____

_____

_____

64

Why We Worry and How to Control It

"Worry never robs tomorrow of its sorrow,
it only saps today of its joy."
~Leo Buscaglia

Ironically, worrying, which is typically an attempt to antici-pate and prevent bad things happening, tends to make one even more anxious, creating a never-ending and escalating cycle of anxiety–worry–more anxiety–more worry–etc. First and foremost, we fear the future. Some worrying and concern for the future may be unavoidable and, in certain situations, necessary and potentially helpful. However, in essence our nonstop worrying has made us sick.

So what is the solution to the dilemma of worry being such a common facet of our lives? Cognitive–behavioral ther-apy helps patients to see that their worrying is irrational and counterproductive. Existential psychiatrist Victor Frankl em-ployed a technique he called "paradoxical intention"; rather than worrying about controlling and concealing your anxiety, willing instead to be as anxious as possible in certain nerve-wracking contexts can paradoxically decrease your situational anxiety and worry. Here are six techniques to help you stop worrying about things you can't control:

1. Determine what you can control. Recognize that sometimes all you can control is your reaction and

your own attitude. When you put your energy into the things you can control, you will be more effective.

2. Focus on your influence. To have the most influence, focus on changing your behavior.
3. Identify your fears. Acknowledging that you can handle the worst-case scenario can help you put your energy into more productive areas.
4. Differentiate between ruminating and problem solving. Ask yourself whether your thinking is productive and only keep thinking if you are working on an actual solution.
5. Create a plan to manage your stress. Find healthy stress relievers like those outlined in this book. Pay attention to your stress level, and notice how you cope with the stress. Eliminate unhealthy coping skills, like complaining or using unhealthy substances.
6. Develop healthy affirmations. Use quick, little phrases that remind you either to take action or to calm down.

Reflections

_____

_____

_____

_____

_____

_____

_____

_____

_____

_____

_____

65

The Four Agreements

In 1997, Don Miquel Ruiz published the book *The Four Agreements*. The simple ideas of *The Four Agreements* provide an inspirational code for life, a personal development model, and a template for personal development, behavior, communications, and relationships. A summary of Don Miguel Ruiz's four agreements:

1. Be impeccable with your word – speak with integrity. Say only what you mean. Avoid using words to speak against yourself or to gossip about others. Use the power of your word in the direction of truth and love.
2. Don't take anything personally – nothing others do is because of you. What others say and do are projections of their own reality. When you are immune to the opinions and actions of others, you won't be the victim of needless suffering.
3. Don't make assumptions – find the courage to ask questions and to express what you really want. Communicate with others as clearly as you can to avoid misunderstandings, sadness, and drama.
4. Always do your best – your best is going to change from moment to moment; it will be different when you are healthy as opposed to not feeling well. Under any circumstance, simply do your best, and you will avoid self-judgment, self-abuse, and regret.

Reflections

_____

_____

_____

_____

_____

_____

_____

_____

_____

_____

_____

66

Start New Habits that Actually Stick

"Your beliefs become your thoughts,
your thoughts become your words,
your words become your actions,
your actions become your habits,
your habits become your values,
and your values become your destiny."
~Mahatma Gandhi

Every habit you have—good or bad—follows the same three-step pattern.

1. Reminder – the trigger that initiates the behavior. A good reminder makes it easy to start by encoding your new behavior in something that you already do. For example, to create a new habit of flossing, always do it after brushing your teeth.

2. Routine – the behavior itself, the action you take. It is important to remember that lasting change is the product of daily habits, not once-in-a-lifetime trans-formations. You must start small. You may try asking yourself, "How can I make this new behavior so easy to do that I can't say no?"

3. Reward – the benefit you gain from doing the be-havior. Always give yourself credit and enjoy each

success. It is important to celebrate each action toward your new habit.

This book combines the many practices of mindfulness (embracing the power of the present), tips on how to harness the power of your own mind, and how to make changes in our mind. The fact is, we have all we need to make any necessary changes to better our lives without changing external circumstances per se. The future is the result of what we do right now, and the reality is: Now is the only time! In the words of a great Buddhist teacher, Pema Chodron, "How we relate to the now creates the future."

The number sixty-six is in the title and a prominent feature of this book as it relates to the actual number of days it takes to create a new habit. While this process may vary by individual, the only way to get to day sixty-six or day five hundred is to start with day one. My sincere hope and wish for each reader is that this book inspires that individual to take the challenge to embrace the "now," to realize that the most potent changes start within, and to be inspired by the information contained in this book to begin to take the power of change and happiness into his or her own hands.

Implementations

_____

_____

_____

_____

_____

_____

_____

_____

_____

_____

_____

_____

_____

_____

_____

_____

_____

_____

_____

_____

_____

_____

_____

About the Author

Pamela Michelle, J.D., M.S., graduated with honors from the University of Florida (B.A., Political Science) before entering law school at age twenty. Obtaining her Juris Doctorate in 1991, she was admitted to both the Georgia Bar and the Florida Bar. Through 1996 she was defense counsel for corporations in injury litigation and labor/civil rights cases. For the past twenty-one years, she has served in these same areas as plaintiffs' counsel. After working in two large law firms, she opened her own practice in 2012.

Pam obtained her M.S. in mental health counseling in 2004 and has completed more than one thousand therapy hours assisting clients. Certified as a coach by the International Coaching Federation, she shares her coaching and consulting practice with individuals from all walks of life.

Pam has done intensive study under numerous masters of ancient wisdom, neuroscience, philosophy, world religions, indigenous and sacred traditions, and mindfulness/insight practices. She continues on this path as a lifelong learner, seeker, advisor, and teacher. Incorporating a passion for transpersonal, humanistic, and existential perspectives into her work, her worldview has unfolded through extensive travel and a constant quest for self-actualization.

Pam's greatest passion is to help others "deep-dive" into their own inner being, allowing the radiant beauty of their soul's purpose to emerge into the world, resulting in self-fulfillment and a calming sense of wholeness. The goal she envisions is for them to achieve a profound alchemical transformation of consciousness.

As the founder and CEO of SoulofLawyers.com, the Soul of Lawyers Network, and PamelaMichelle.com, Pam offers platforms for coaching, consulting, speaking, sacred travel, and networking opportunities.

She is the co-author of Amazon's best-selling book, *Women Who Inspire.*

Pam can be contacted at Pam@Pamelamichelle.com or Pam@souloflawyers.com.